Gestalt
Therapy

Theories of Psychotherapy Series

Theories of Psychotherapy Series
Jon Carlson and Matt Englar-Carlson, Series Editors

Gestalt Therapy

Gordon Wheeler and Lena Axelsson

American Psychological Association

Washington, DC

Published by
American Psychological Association
750 First Street, NE
Washington, DC 20002
www.apa.org

To order
APA Order Department
P.O. Box 92984
Washington, DC 20090-2984
Tel: (800) 374-2721; Direct: (202) 336-5510
Fax: (202) 336-5502; TDD/TTY: (202) 336-6123
Online: www.apa.org/pubs/books
E-mail: order@apa.org

In the U.K., Europe, Africa, and the Middle East, copies may be ordered from
American Psychological Association
3 Henrietta Street
Covent Garden, London
WC2E 8LU England

Typeset in Minion by Circle Graphics, Inc., Columbia, MD

Printer: Edwards Brothers Malloy, Inc., Lillington, NC
Cover Designer: Minker Design, Sarasota, FL
Cover Art: *Lily Rising,* 2005, oil and mixed media on panel in craquelure frame, by Betsy Bauer

The opinions and statements published are the responsibility of the authors, and such opinions and statements do not necessarily represent the policies of the American Psychological Association.

Library of Congress Cataloging-in-Publication Data

Wheeler, Gordon, 1949-
  Gestalt therapy / by Gordon Wheeler & Lena Axelsson. — First edition.
      pages cm. — (Theories of psychotherapy series)
  Includes bibliographical references and index.
  ISBN 978-1-4338-1859-2 — ISBN 1-4338-1859-0 1. Gestalt therapy. I. Axelsson, Lena. II. Title.
  RC489.G4W44 2015
  616.89'143—dc23
                              2014032667

British Library Cataloguing-in-Publication Data
A CIP record is available from the British Library.

Printed in the United States of America
First Edition

http://dx.doi.org/10.1037/14527-000

Contents

Series Preface

Some might argue that in the contemporary clinical practice of psycho-therapy, evidence-based intervention and effective outcome have overshadowed theory in importance. Maybe. But, as the editors of this series, we don't propose to take up that controversy here. We do know that psychotherapists adopt and practice according to one theory or another because their experience, and decades of good evidence, suggests that having a sound theory of psychotherapy leads to greater therapeutic success. Still, the role of theory in the helping process can be hard to explain. This narrative about solving problems helps convey theory's importance:

> Aesop tells the fable of the sun and wind having a contest to decide
> who was the most powerful. From above the earth, they spotted a
> man walking down the street, and the wind said that he bet he could
> get his coat off. The sun agreed to the contest. The wind blew, and the
> man held on tightly to his coat. The more the wind blew, the tighter
> he held. The sun said it was his turn. He put all of his energy into
> creating warm sunshine, and soon the man took off his coat.

What does a competition between the sun and the wind to remove a man's coat have to do with theories of psychotherapy? We think this deceptively simple story highlights the importance of theory as the precursor to any effective intervention—and hence to a favorable outcome. Without a guiding theory we might treat the symptom without understanding the role of the individual. Or we might create power conflicts with our clients and not understand that, at times, indirect means of helping (sunshine) are often as effective—if not more so—than direct ones (wind). In the absence of theory, we might lose track of the treatment rationale and instead get caught up in, for example, social correctness and not wanting to do something that looks too simple.

What exactly *is* theory? The *APA Dictionary of Psychology* defines theory as "a principle or body of interrelated principles that purports to explain or predict a number of interrelated phenomena." In psychotherapy, a theory is a set of principles used to explain human thought and behavior, including what causes people to change. In practice, a theory creates the goals of therapy and specifies how to pursue them. Haley (1997) noted that a theory of psychotherapy ought to be simple enough for the average therapist to understand, but comprehensive enough to account for a wide range of eventualities. Furthermore, a theory guides action toward successful outcomes while generating hope in both the therapist and client that recovery is possible.

Theory is the compass that allows psychotherapists to navigate the vast territory of clinical practice. In the same ways that navigational tools have been modified to adapt to advances in thinking and ever-expanding territories to explore, theories of psychotherapy have changed over time. The different schools of theories are commonly referred to as waves, the first wave being psychodynamic theories (i.e., Adlerian, psychoanalytic), the second wave learning theories (i.e., behavioral, cognitive–behavioral), the third wave humanistic theories (person-centered, gestalt, existential), the fourth wave feminist and multicultural theories, and the fifth wave postmodern and constructivist theories. In many ways, these waves represent how psychotherapy has adapted and responded to changes in psychology, society, and epistemology as well as to changes in the nature of psychotherapy itself. Psychotherapy and the theories that guide it are dynamic and responsive. The wide variety of theories is also testament to the different ways in which the same human behavior can be conceptualized (Frew & Spiegler, 2008).

It is with these two concepts in mind—the central importance of theory and the natural evolution of theoretical thinking—that we developed the APA Theories of Psychotherapy Series. Both of us are thoroughly fascinated by theory and the range of complex ideas that drive each model. As university faculty members who teach courses on the theories of psychotherapy, we wanted to create learning materials that not only highlight the essence of the major theories for professionals and professionals in training but also clearly bring the reader up to date on the current status of the models. Often in books on theory, the biography of the original theorist overshadows the evolution of the model. In contrast, our intent is to highlight the contemporary uses of the theories as well as their history and context.

As this project began, we faced two immediate decisions: which theories to address and who best to present them. We looked at graduate-level theories of psychotherapy courses to see which theories are being taught, and we explored popular scholarly books, articles, and conferences to determine which theories draw the most interest. We then developed a dream list of authors from among the best minds in contemporary theoretical practice. Each author is one of the leading proponents of that approach as well as a knowledgeable practitioner. We asked each author to review the core constructs of the theory, bring the theory into the modern sphere of clinical practice by looking at it through a context of evidence-based practice, and clearly illustrate how the theory looks in action.

There are 24 titles planned for the series. Each title can stand alone or can be put together with a few other titles to create materials for a course in psychotherapy theories. This option allows instructors to create a course featuring the approaches they believe are the most salient today. To support this end, APA Books has also developed a DVD for each of the approaches that demonstrates the theory in practice with a real client. Many of the DVDs show therapy over six sessions. Contact APA Books for a complete list of available DVD programs (http://www.apa.org/pubs/videos).

Gestalt therapy is an experiential and existential form of psychotherapy that highlights the present moment and personal responsibility with the goal of helping clients become more alive. Many contemporary theories utilize Gestalt therapy techniques; however, few clinicians understand the theoretical roots of this approach and these interventions. In this book, Gordon Wheeler and Lena Axelsson share their thorough knowledge of the theoretical underpinnings of this complete contemporary system of psychotherapy. They cleverly invite the reader to participate in a conversation about the origins and philosophy of Gestalt as well as its modern application. We include this important approach in the Theories of Psychotherapy series in the hope that readers can understand this approach and its application to a wide range of challenges involved with modern life.

—Jon Carlson and Matt Englar-Carlson

REFERENCES

Frew, J., & Spiegler, M. (2008). *Contemporary psychotherapies for a diverse world*. Boston, MA: Lahaska Press.

Haley, J. (1997). *Leaving home: The therapy of disturbed young people*. New York, NY: Routledge.

How to Use This Book With APA Psychotherapy Videos

Each book in the *Theories of Psychotherapy Series* is specifically paired with a DVD that demonstrates the theory applied in actual therapy with a real client. Many DVDs feature the author of the book as the guest therapist, allowing students to see an eminent scholar and practitioner putting the theory they write about into action.

The DVDs have a number of features that make them excellent tools for learning more about theoretical concepts:

- Many DVDs contain six full sessions of psychotherapy over time, giving viewers a chance to see how clients respond to the application of the theory over the course of several sessions.
- Each DVD has a brief introductory discussion recapping the basic features of the theory behind the approach demonstrated. This allows viewers to review the key aspects of the approach about which they have just read.
- DVDs feature actual clients in unedited psychotherapy sessions. This provides a unique opportunity to get a sense of the look and feel of real psychotherapy, something that written case examples and transcripts sometimes cannot convey.
- There is a therapist commentary track that viewers may choose to play during the psychotherapy sessions. This track gives unique insight into why therapists do what they do in a session. Further it provides an

in vivo opportunity to see how the therapist uses the model to conceptualize the client.

The books and DVDs together make a powerful teaching tool for showing how theoretical principles affect practice. In the case of this book, the DVD *Gestalt Therapy*, which features Dr. Wheeler as the guest expert, provides a vivid example of how this approach looks in practice.

Acknowledgments

My thanks go first of all to my coauthor, Lena Axelsson: Without your energy, creative drive, and the fresh imagination you bring of a new generation of Gestaltists and healers, this book would never have come to fruition. Growing older I become ever more mindful of existing as part of a unified web of giving and receiving, which underlies and empowers all our actions, experiences, and coevolution. The great benefit of long life is having the chance to love, learn from, nourish and be nourished by so many people. Thanks go to all my teachers, mentors, colleagues, students, sparring partners, clients, friends and family, children and grandchildren, for being the people I continue to learn from and learn with—and to my teachers and mentors in Gestalt, themselves direct students of Kurt Lewin, Paul Goodman, and Fritz and Laura Perls, to whom I dedicate my work in this book.

—Gordon Wheeler

I would like to start by thanking my coauthor, Gordon Wheeler, not only for asking me to write this book with him but mostly for the many years of mentorship and friendship he has provided. I also want to thank Helen Resneck-Sannes for her support in helping me understand not only intellectually but in my own body the effects trauma has on a cellular level.

Thank you also to my colleagues at the Gestalt Academy of Scandinavia, especially Helena Kallner and Petra Juneholm, for your support through this process, and to my friends who have encouraged and supported me especially during the times when I was questioning my abilities to reach the end of the journey of writing this book.

I want to also acknowledge the psychotherapists at PVPSA (Pajaro Valley Prevention and Student Assistance in Watsonville, CA)—my former coworkers and supervisees, especially Diana Ramirez-Zuniga, who was the family therapist on two of the cases presented in this book. You are all doing such amazing work bringing help and support to children and families who have no means of getting help in any other way, working from a true field perspective and always looking at how to expand the support for each client outside of the therapy room. Finally, I offer special thanks to my teachers and mentors in Gestalt, and to my students, to whom I dedicate my work in this book.

—*Lena Axelsson*

Gestalt Therapy

1

Introduction

Welcome to this book on Gestalt therapy. Our aim in writing it has been to give you, the reader, an overview of the theory and the philosophy and values behind it, as well as a sense of how Gestalt therapy is practiced. We hope you will find it an interesting and worthwhile read, one that will give you not only a good introductory view of Gestalt therapy theory and practice but also a new perspective on what it means to be a therapist, no matter what school of thought you practice from.

Gestalt therapy is a distinct therapeutic approach in its own right, and at the same time the psychological theory behind Gestalt therapy has had a far-reaching influence on other schools of research psychology in the past century; thus, we believe (and hope to convince you here) that many of the basic assumptions of Gestalt can clarify and support your learning and growth in any therapeutic model and methodology. This is especially true when it comes to how Gestalt therapy views the importance of the

http://dx.doi.org/10.1037/14527-001
Gestalt Therapy, by G. Wheeler and L. Axelsson

therapist–client relationship for the client's healing and growth and how Gestalt therapists work from a profoundly phenomenological approach, grounded in the firm, research-backed idea that that each of us is engaged at every moment in life in a unique project of creating our own view and understanding of reality. In Gestalt, it is this creative human process of meaning making, shared and at the same time unique to each of us, which is the focus in therapy.

AUDIENCE

As authors, we always have in mind the question of who our audience may be as we write. Many of our readers, we know, will be students and trainees in psychotherapy and related fields (counseling, coaching, group and organizational work, and increasingly, working with teams, communities, and policy issues). Thus, we have done our best, using a diverse variety of case examples and settings, to convey a hands-on feel for how Gestalt therapy works in practice, hopefully bringing the theory discussions to life in a way you can relate to, find yourself in, and adapt creatively to your own needs. We believe Gestalt has much to offer as you clarify and deepen your own source models and your own work, just as we have learned over the years from a wide range of teachers and approaches, often adapting ideas from other schools to specifically challenging clients and populations—without leaving our "home" orientation and theory perspective in relational Gestalt.

Therapists and related professionals are lifelong learners, always looking for new tools, new ideas, and new opportunities for personal and professional growth to help us meet the challenges coming from our clients, our projects, our personal relationships—and ourselves. This should not be surprising, because as members of the helping professions, we take as our study area nothing less than the most complex process system in the known universe: a human relationship. How human beings work, how we live in and emerge from a "relational ground" from before birth and all through life (and in some sense beyond), is the subject matter of Gestalt therapy and the source of our theories and methods for being of more service to other people (clients and others)—and to ourselves.

WHO WE ARE

Diversity (and connection) is the dual nature of life—between group and group and also between any two individuals: In today's multicultural world, none of us can afford not to be mindful of how group membership and identification affect each and all of us in every situation—including the therapist–client relationship. Thus, we, the coauthors, want readers to know something about our own backgrounds. As well as in other important ways, we are alike in that we both come from the generally privileged North Atlantic community of nations (Europe and North America), and we have both had the blessing of the opportunity for a high-quality education. Beyond that, one of us is of Caucasian origin, the other Caucasian plus Native American. We are of different genders and from different generations, with different cultures of origin and different primary languages. But we are joined in a passionate commitment to Gestalt therapy as the most useful basic framework and tool we have come across for studying relationships, and we are joined in our commitment to being of service to a wide range of people as they address the challenges of their lives.

OVERVIEW OF THIS BOOK

Every method, every school of therapy, rests on an underlying theory and set of assumptions (spoken or unspoken) about human nature. Underlying Gestalt therapy is the research-based theory of Gestalt psychology—a basic model and research core that has come to inform the assumptions and underlying concepts of most modern research psychology (including the contemporary revolution in neuroscience and interpersonal neurobiology, about which we will have much more to say later in the volume). Because the roots and essential connections between this Gestalt psychology legacy and the later (midcentury) emergence of Gestalt therapy have often been underdiscussed or misunderstood, we spend some time in Chapter 2 showing you the basics of that earlier Gestalt psychology model and how it gave rise to Gestalt therapy after decades of basic lab and social research. That Gestalt psychology revolution of a century ago first challenged and then came to underlie and unify the other two great rival schools (or families of schools) we know as *behaviorism* and *psycho-dynamics.* This deeper shared ground among all three of these movements (behavioral; psychodynamic; and *relational/humanistic,* of which Gestalt therapy is a part) is also not always understood in the (sometimes) contentious wider field of psychology and psychotherapy, and we hope you will find the discussion here to be lively and of value to you in locating and clarifying your own assumptions and perspective.

In Chapter 3, we take up the emergence of Gestalt therapy—its theory and its evolution over the past six and more decades. We round out that discussion with an overview of contemporary relational Gestalt theory and practice, as we understand and articulate it. In Chapter 4, we take this theory into the therapy room, highlighting the practice of relational Gestalt therapy with a number of diverse case studies (diverse demographically, and with regard to age, setting, presenting problem and issues, and mode of therapy). As we introduce the case vignette we insert our initials, respectively, to identify the therapist/speaker in that case. We move on in Chapter 5 to current outcome research on Gestalt and closely related methods. Although outcome research on Gestalt therapy per se has so far been limited, we argue that the more extensive research on relationally oriented therapy in general is directly relevant. Even more, across the field of outcome research in psychotherapy the evidence emerges again and again (even in cases in which the research focus was initially different) that the most consistently important, repeatedly recurring factors in successful therapeutic outcomes have to do with the basic Gestalt tenet of the importance of the dynamics and qualities of the therapeutic relationship. Indeed, in this chapter and throughout this volume, we argue that in Gestalt therapy the client–therapist relationship *is* the therapy in some real senses. We hope that by the end of this volume you will have a feel for what we mean by this.

In Chapter 6, we examine the trajectory we believe relational Gestalt therapy will take in the coming years, which will be a time of continuing and amazing ferment and transformation in psychology in general, thanks to the neuroscience revolution that is today only still dawning. We relate that revolution to ongoing developments we foresee in Gestalt therapy in general, in trauma healing in particular, and in the widespread and growing awareness that psychotherapy must move beyond the therapy room and integrate with the larger field of community, educational, and family needs and support.

In Chapter 7, we sum up this journey, in hopes that we have contributed something to your own journey as a student, trainee, or active professional already in the field. To accommodate the relatively brief space of this volume, we have made many difficult choices about what to delve into deeply and what to touch on lightly. We have so much to tell you, and we sense that we can only give you a taste here of the whole rich menu of Gestalt. Therefore, we hope that you will continue your studies in Gestalt therapy using the Suggested Reading section at the end of this book.

Finally, a note on the use of the pronouns *you*, *we*, and *us*. We view writing a book as a way of opening a conversation with you, the reader—albeit only half a dialogue for now, because this is in book form. Thus, we invite and welcome your comments, questions, requests for further reading, and so forth (see the e-mail addresses in each of our bios). Meanwhile, we hope this way of writing will invite you to explore your own process of meaning making and your thoughts, feelings, and sensations as you read. Blessings to you on your journey as you learn, grow, serve, and help to heal others and yourselves.

2

History

A century ago, when psychology was still in its infancy, a group of young academic researchers in Berlin set out to explore a set of old problems in a radically new way. In the view of this renegade group, soon to be known as *Gestaltists* or the *Gestalt school*, the prevailing approach of the times to a scientific understanding of perception, cognition, and ultimately human experience and behavior was fundamentally too limited; a new beginning was needed. The issues at stake were among the most daunting and significant involving human nature; namely, how do we actually take in, know, and use our world? How do human perception, cognition, behavior, motivation, experience, and so forth, actually work?

Centuries of speculative philosophy (the branch known as *philosophy of mind*) had wrestled deeply with these questions, with whole schools of thought emerging based on speculation and imagined models of explanation. Formalists or *idealists* (who held that the mind is preorganized by

http://dx.doi.org/10.1037/14527-002
Gestalt Therapy, by G. Wheeler and L. Axelsson

fixed, innate structures) had vied for centuries with empiricists or *realists* (who believed that the mind is a "blank slate," merely the sum of sense impressions; Russell, 1946/2004), with no clear result. By the turn of the 20th century the new philosophical school of *phenomenology* was trying to renew the discussion by reflecting deeply on experience, but this approach was highly subjective and speculative and thus not in tune with the era's vigorous empirical research in physics, chemistry, physiology, and related fields (Husserl, 1928/1990). In the second half of the 19th century the legacy of philosophy of mind had birthed an entirely new offshoot: *scientific psychology*, the empirical, experiment-based study of human behavior and experience taking the mind as a research topic and using the new tools and methods of modern empirical science to try to unravel mysteries that had fascinated (and often stumped) the best minds of the past 2,500 years of the Western philosophical tradition.

THE AGE OF ENGINEERING: ASSOCIATIONISM AND THE WORK OF THE FIRST PSYCHOLOGISTS

The end of the 19th century was the dawn of the great modern age of science and technology, a time of vast optimism in scientific circles and beyond. In the late 19th century, amazing new advances in physics and chemistry—from molecular and atomic theory to the germ theory of disease to applications such as the harnessing of electricity, the radio and the telephone, the first automobiles and then airplanes, and so much more—seemed to promise that nature's power and secrets would soon be solidly under human control. And because the new theories of Darwin were placing humans fully in the natural world, surely human behavior and the human mind could likewise be unlocked, understood scientifically, and reshaped for human betterment.

It was in this spirit of self-confidence and faith in science that the first research labs in psychology were founded in 1879 in Leipzig, Germany, by the great pioneer of psychological research, Wilhelm Wundt, founder of modern psychology as a research-based discipline (Wundt, 1904/2009). Following the lead of the physical sciences of the day, the research approach was resolutely *atomistic*—that is, the methodology involved breaking down the complex mysteries of activities such as perception, cognition, and behavior into what surely must be their simplest basic units. The approach was similar to those of physics and chemistry in material science, reducing complex substances and reactions to the basic building blocks of molecules and atoms and then recording their properties and interactions to "build up" again into larger understandings that would explain and predict the natural world (Wundt, 1904/2009). The approach was grounded in the exciting new work of Pavlov (1897) on the stimulus–response (S–R) bond. The awarding of the 1906 Nobel Prize in Medicine to Pavlov for this work provided, at the most scientifically prestigious level, a kind of official endorsement of this way of thinking.

As Wundt and his group imagined it, perception and cognition could be understood by measuring and administering the smallest possible unit of a physical *stimulus* (e.g., minimal increments of heat, light, sound, skin pressure, electrical impulse) to a participant in the lab and then tracking and measuring the physiological *response* (not the "whole-person" or full behavioral response but first the microreaction at the level of the nervous system, exact physical measurements such as muscle movement, nerve impulse, retinal or aural reaction, voltaic potential changes on the surface of the skin, etc.; see Wheeler, 2000; Wundt, 1904/2009).

Certainly Wundt and his followers understood that research at this level was still far removed from the ultimate goal of understanding and predicting changes in behavior and consciousness. But those larger processes, they felt, must surely be made up in some direct way of *associative chains* of smaller, concrete S–R events. As long as the researchers stayed faithful to their principles of concrete physical data with no speculation or imposition of any imaginary ideas, their theory would be as solid as the material physics of their day, the great Newtonian synthesis, augmented by 19th-century chemistry and atom theory, which was transforming the physical world around them. In this way, the new field of psychology took its place alongside the other empirical sciences, with the same status and the same explanatory power and limitless applications for societal issues, education, and social engineering.

This was the vision on which psychology had been founded only a few decades before. The idea of associative chains gave the new research movement its name: *associationism*, or the *associationist school* in the new psychology. By the turn of the 20th century—which is to say just a single generation after the founding of research psychology as a discipline— associationism had outpaced its more speculative rivals, amassing huge quantities of basic S–R data and arriving at a neurological understanding of the human nervous system and how it works, at least at the most basic physical response level, information that today remains fundamental in modern behaviorism, much of learning theory, and the foundations of neuroscience, even if the conceptual model of associationism no longer serves as a basic framework of psychology (Boring, 1950).

Despite the productivity and usefulness of the first generation of basic associationist research, the original aims of the field—a fuller understanding of higher order phenomena such as consciousness, behavior, and how the mind actually works—seemed no closer than before to any useful answers. If anything, the mystery surrounding these larger questions seemed only to grow deeper the more the basic building blocks of perception in the form of S–R links accumulated, without any clear way to get from these basics to a fuller, empirically tested model of how the larger processes work.

ASSOCIATIONISM AND ITS CRITICS: THE UNANSWERED QUESTIONS

From its beginnings, associationism did not lack doubters and critics. Prominent among them was the great American psychologist William James, widely recognized today as the founder of American psychology (James, 1890/2007). James, who had a European education, had studied for a time as a young man at the Wundt labs in Leipzig soon after their founding and had come away dissatisfied. The problem, as he later put it, was that although we are certainly being bombarded at every moment by a near infinitude of stimuli, how do human beings ever actually get out of that raw stimulus world of "blooming, buzzing confusion" (James, 1890/2007, p. 488) to the manifestly organized, coherent, and above all, usable world of perceptions, cognitions, and useful learning, leading at least at times to reflection and learning, evaluation and perhaps prediction, and then to strategies, integration, and even the sensation at least of making judgments and choice?

All this amassing of S–R data, James argued, was missing the real question of perception (James, 1890/2007; see also Wheeler, 2000). One does need to know about atoms to understand the physical world, but just counting atoms and then adding them up in chains—even all the atoms in the universe, if that were possible—would not do the whole job. The problem is much more complex: One also needs to know the *principles of interaction*, which include the laws of attraction and which atoms do what and under what conditions. In the same way, the problem of perception, according to James (1890/2007), could never be explained away by simply registering and measuring all the physical sense impressions and then associating one S–R pairing with another in some linear way—if only because the stimuli around us, at a physical level, are essentially infinite and always changing (utterly unlike the static world of the Wundt labs with their carefully measured doses of single stimuli).

Each perceiving subject has to have some criteria for relevance and selection and some principles of construction and integration to get out of the chaos of pure stimulus and into organized, selected, and usable perceptions. Out of the infinitude of all the energy impulses that are assaulting you at every waking moment, which stimuli matter? How would you select among them (and even more important, deselect or screen out the majority of them—and keep doing so all the time as your only possible defense against being overwhelmed)? Under what circumstances would you not pay attention to different aspects of the environment under different conditions (a key point that would only begin to be clarified with the work of Gestaltist Kurt Lewin a generation later, as we will see later in the chapter)? Once we have selected or deselected, how do we make a coherent whole picture of all those elements we have somehow "screened in." Associationism seemed to have no answers to offer to questions such as these.

James (1890/2007) proposed studying attention, specifically *selective attention*, as he termed it. Otherwise one would be left with an unbridgeable gap between sensory data and S–R cataloging and the actual emergence of a coherent perceptual image, cognition, or memory—much less anything such as a full account of learning and judgment and their role in behavior. Atomism and associationism alone could never accomplish this; something more would always be needed for a coherent, scientific, and ultimately predictive explanation (and prediction, after all, is the gold standard of science). What that "something more" is and how to describe it James left for other scholars to work out. But without that inquiry and a fuller theory, the gap between empirical research and a fully articulated, fully usable model remained and even seemed to widen.

THE GESTALT PSYCHOLOGY AGENDA: THE WORK OF THE FIRST GESTALT GENERATION

It was into that gap—the unexplored expanse between the static, simpler S–R world of the associationists and the dynamic, complex world of the actual, purposive responses that make up our experience and our behavior—that this intrepid new group of young psychologists in Berlin, the first Gestalt psychologists, beginning in the early years of the 20th century, were determined to go. Like the philosophers who searched for "mental categories" from Plato to Kant to Husserl down to the new phenomenologists of that day (Brentano, 1988; Husserl, 1928/1990; Kant, 1781/1983), they would be exploring the larger organizing principles and dynamics of perception and cognition. The idea was to fill in that gap between environmental stimulus and behavioral response with clear principles, mechanisms, and demonstrable "laws" (like the S–R bond but with greater complexity) that might get us more persuasively from "input" to "output."

Unlike the more traditional reflective philosophers, the Gestaltists explored these questions empirically, using the methods and tools of the new psychology labs: controlled measurement, repeatable trials, hypothesis formation, and hypothesis testing, followed by model building on the bases of those hypotheses that had survived the fire of rigorous testing. In this way they built on Wundt's innovation of applying the tools and methods of the physical sciences to psychological research; only in place of the discrete physical stimulus or doses and the measurement sensory reactions, thresholds, and response times of much of the Wundt lab's work, they turned their focus to the behavioral response of the whole perceiving subject, dealing with some perceptual scene or situation and responding to the image or pattern as a whole.

As experimental variables they used visual or auditory presentations, often some incomplete or ambiguous sequence or image—all those relatively more lifelike situations and presentations that challenge an active subject to learn or use something, recognize on the basis of incomplete cues, or make a judgment, a discrimination, or other choice. They were trying to solve the mystery of selection, deselection, and above all, synthesizing that James had pointed to, in search of those unifying principles (Wertheimer, 1912) that would transform the sheer perceptual inputs or stimulus events of much of the Wundt lab's research into some whole coherent picture or recognition (something like the famous "Aha!" reaction that is popularly associated with much of this early Gestalt thinking and research; Wertheimer, 1925, 1938). They took their name, *Gestaltists* and *Gestalt psychology*, from the term introduced into research as early as the 1890s by Ehrenfels (1890) to indicate this unifying phenomenon, which was still missing but now named as a research topic (*Gestalt* is simply a German word signifying form or whole configuration).

One might think (as many associationists did) that this "how" question, being invisible and thus perhaps speculative, would be nearly impossible to pin down in the lab. And yet, in an outpouring of creativity, the initial Gestalt research team led by Max Wertheimer, Kurt Koffka, Wolfgang von Köhler, and their associates (Henle, 1961), in just a few years before the outbreak of World War I, generated a wealth of new experimental directions and findings casting light on just these yet-invisible processes. The findings soon confirmed not just the existence but also the active role of these selective and integrative mental processes in mediating behavior; they at least began to describe the workings and the principles governing "in-brain" processes in well-researched detail. (For a broad sweep of this first decade's work, see the primary research in Ellis, 1938, and Henle, 1961; see also Wheeler, 2000.)

Often the specific experiments that they came up with were probing and quite ingenious. One elegant, deceptively simple example was based on the research carried out by Pavlov (1897), who trained people (or dogs, or birds) to always associate a given stimulus—a simple disc image, say—with some reward (generally food, if working with animals). The picture was then complicated, first by presenting the subjects with a choice between two discs (e.g., 1 inch and 2 inches), and pairing only one of them with the reward. Even a chicken would soon learn to reliably choose and pick on the correct disc (e.g., the larger, 2-inch disc) most of the time, ignoring the other one and getting the reward.

And then the task was complicated further: Once the animals were trained on the 2-inch disc, the stimuli were changed again, the ignored (and irrelevant) 1-inch disc was removed, and the same subjects were presented with the same 2-inch disc—only now paired with, for example, a 4-inch disc in place of the smaller one. Would the participants now pick the same 2-inch disc as before (as the associationist model would certainly predict—the "correct" physical stimulus has not changed in all this time), or would they now choose the *larger* of the two (i.e., the 4-inch disc), just as they had been picking the larger one (i.e., the 2-inch disc) in the previous training phase? This is an ingenious way of ascertaining what the participant was actually learning: whether absolute size (always the same 2-inch disc) or relative size (the larger of any two) was related to the likelihood of reward.

If it turned out (as it often did) to be the latter (i.e., they had actually been learning to choose the larger stimulus—a *relative* discrimination, not a simple one-to-one stimulus training), then the result was not simply a matter of responding to pure physical stimuli. On the contrary, the participant was making an interpretive judgment call and not a one-to-one direct physical stimulus response. The response was not to the stimulus alone but to the stimulus *in a given context* (the same 2-inch disc may be the larger one in one array and the smaller in another pairing, and subjects would pick it or not, depending on what else it was paired with).

Although this task is a simple perceptual challenge compared with the complex perceptions humans and other animals handle nearly every moment, even at this simple level we can no longer reduce the whole perceptual problem to just a fixed, passive S–R bond or direct physical stimuli; it is clear that the subject is active and is making complex contextual judgments that are "whole-picture" interpretations, more relative (larger, smaller) than absolute (the number and spacing of photons coming from the disc to our retina). These judgments do not occur just *after* the act of perception; they are *part of that perceptual act and process.* With this kind of work, the Gestaltists opened the research field to those internal processes the early behaviorists still hoped to avoid with a pure S–R model. (For this and other such ingenious experiments, again see Ellis, 1938; Henle, 1961; see also Wheeler, 1991.)

Thus the Gestalt revolution in cognitive research began. Not only did these findings (and many more, many of them equally ingenious) hold up under repeated trials, but the Gestaltists also found that subjects could be presented with more and more difficult challenges, such as smaller and smaller size discriminations or keeping the "same" stimulus in entirely different situations, and give *different* responses to the *same* physical input (e.g., participants could be asked to label the same object with the same objective brightness as either *white* or *black*, depending on the overall lighting and shading of the whole scene, and still get reliable, repeatable and surprising patterns of results; see Köhler, 1938a; Wheeler, 1991).

Another classic example, even more familiar and seemingly simple, is a melody. How is it that we can recognize what we call "the same tune" no matter what note it starts on or what key it then unfolds in? How can that be, if we are presumably just responding directly to the physical stimulus of the absolute frequencies of the notes? Clearly, what we are governed by here is not any one frequency or note but the melody as a whole—that is, the whole pattern or the relative intervals of frequencies (or the relative spaces *between* notes—i.e., the places where there is *no* physical stimulus—that are regulating the response). Again, a reductive S–R or associationist approach seems to have little to offer in pattern-recognition problems such as this. And yet, all perception, all recognition, involves pattern recognition in some way, to varying degrees (Ehrenfels, 1890).

In another hallmark study in this early Gestalt research, participants were forced into discrimination or judgment challenges through the use of ambiguous or incomplete images (or images containing intentional errors); experimenters registered the perceptual patterns and biases that emerged as they manipulated experimental variables such as time, light, focus, inclusion or exclusion of important elements of detail, differing or competing contexts, and so forth (e.g., the optical illusions or ambiguous images often found in textbook illustrations of early Gestalt work). From this they began to collect and catalog the perceptual biases and tendencies that would go into the early Gestalt principles of perception (Wertheimer, 1925, 1938). The following is a brief outline with commentary of the most important of these principles—radical at the time, familiar (if still challenging) today, in a world where these ideas are now the bedrock of contemporary psychology and the ongoing revolution in neuroscience, brain modeling, and the exciting new field of interpersonal neurobiology (Siegel, 2012).

- We tend to perceive in whole forms more than in the actual constituent parts. It is these organized patterns that we can resolve into organized whole images, series, or linkages that the human brain picks out, takes in, stores in memory (or not), and then integrates, where we can, with other perceptions and broader learning. This is the first and fundamental discovery and principle of the Gestalt psychology legacy from the first half of the 20th century (and which laid the groundwork for Gestalt therapy, in ways we will see in the pages to follow).
- These whole forms (or gestalts) are organized according to particular principles, which became known as *Gestalt laws of perception* (Köhler, 1938b; Wertheimer, 1925, 1938; Young, 1999). These principles included such whole-form characteristics as *boundary* (forms or patterns showing borders contrasting with the background), *similarity* (parts of the perceptual field showing repeating features), *contiguity* (nearness vs. distance), *continuity* and *closure* (forms that are unbroken), and so forth, which could then be researched empirically and manipulated experimentally by changing the spacing, timing, contrast, and so on, of the stimuli or by introducing variations, contradictions, or "errors" into a stimulus presentation in the ways described earlier in the "smaller–larger" disc experiments. In a real sense, the stimulus the brain or central nervous system interacts with and responds to is the whole form or pattern and not the various elements that could be shown by other measurements to really exist (Ellis, 1938).

This is fundamental to how we actually function (and to all the Gestalt work up to the present day): The stimulus we see, hear, or otherwise take account of is not the infinity of energy impulses that bombard us but some organized synthesis or reduction of all that into the forms or gestalts our brain and minds are adapted to register and respond to. In other words, in classic Gestalt psychology language, the whole is often more significant than the parts that go into it (e.g., see Koffka, 1935). (For a clear summary of the most important of those Gestalt laws of perception or built-in neurological biases, as we might put it today, see http://web.engr.oregonstate.edu/~sinisa/courses/OSU/CS559/lectures/CS559_1.pdf).

- This then means that perception is active, not passive. Just as William James pointed out, nature simply does not come to us tidily arranged in static, unambiguous, preorganized wholes that we can take as meaningful (in the sense of their being useful to us, having implications, potentially at least, for coping with our situations, surviving in our worlds, and hopefully thriving in our lives). This means we have to select, screen out, emphasize or deemphasize particular features or elements, fill in gaps, leave out contrasting elements, and so forth (all the Gestalt laws of perception in action), to synthesize (and create) and then register images of "what's there" or "what's happening." As Gestaltist Kurt Lewin put it, all perception is a form of problem solving (Marrow, 1969), a proactive process of engaging with our environment to extract and create (and oftentimes modify or distort, as the Gestaltists were showing in "hard," repeatable empirical research) the possible organized forms "out there" that we can remember, relate to, and use in coping with our ever-changing situations and our complex multidimensional lives.

- This also means that there is no perception without interpretation. This is not one of those early laws of perception but rather the direct implication of all those empirical laws taken together. Perception and interpretation are not two completely separate steps (e.g., first I take in what is really there, and only then do I interpret what it means). Rather, we perceive by interpreting (some of) what is there as organized forms

19

and then acting on the basis of that interpretation, not on the basis of completely objective percepts, as the associationists had been assuming. The errors we then make in interpreting cannot be dismissed as just flaws in our human equipment; they are inherent to the perceptual and cognitive process, which is by nature and by necessity a process that is experimental, often rapid, and above all, practical. We scan and integrate and (hopefully) compare and evaluate, all in the service not of "perfect pictures" but practical bases for understanding and action in a dynamic, changing situation.

Again, this is an implication of Gestalt psychology research that later had a direct and transformative impact on psychotherapy; after all, if there is no absolutely objective, finally correct interpretation of perceptions and phenomena and the higher level concepts that emerge from them, what happens to the authoritative interpretations of the classical analyst, which were not offered as interpretations at all in this sense but rather as fixed meanings that the patient had to accept uncritically if she or he were to get better? In the Gestalt psychotherapy model that would emerge from this basic research at mid-century, the old authority basis would shift to a dialogic paradigm, as we see in Chapter 3.

In summary, the human brain is not (as the associationists had assumed) a device for recording reality, at least in any camera-like way. Rather, the human brain and central nervous system form an organ for pattern detection (and pattern creation as well) because it is noticing and creating patterns and whole forms that enable us to adapt to our environment and deal with the ever-changing, ever-new challenges around us. As the creative species par excellence, we need a quick perceptual apparatus that can respond to changing situations, not a stimulus-bound physical response system based on concrete, material S–R bonds alone. Without this essential human interpretive or evaluative step, our behavior cannot be adjusted to our situation; our remarkable capacity for novel, creative responses to new situations, which is our hallmark as humans, would not be possible, and we would be reduced to the mechanistic response to stimuli that is common in the instinctive, largely inflexible response patterns of most other living species. We might never arrive at later stages of reconsideration, checking back, correction, and further levels of integration and learning that we can also attain after the fact, yet are still based on those interpreted perceptions that are the basis of our interactions with our worlds.

Viewed now, nearly a century later, it is easy to see why this basic, research-based conclusion about the fundamental uncertainty of human problem solving, perception, and practical understanding was the most disturbing implication of the new Gestalt perspective, creating controversy at times even among Gestaltists themselves (Gibson, 1950; see also Wheeler, 1991, pp. 66ff). After all, if our perceptions of the world are not just flawed at times but also by their nature always experimental and subjective, never completely objective and stable, then what hope do we have of the kind of absolutely reliable knowledge about our world and ourselves that many were dreaming science would soon be able to provide? (The Gestalt answer to this conundrum of our human condition is deeply dialogic and, in a real sense, intersubjective, in the sense that it is a cocreation between and among individuals, as we will see later and in Chapter 3.)

Meanwhile, James's question and suggested research direction still needed to be addressed. If our perceptions are dependent on context and to that degree are unstable, what is it that determines what we do and do not pay attention to in our over-busy, stimulus-overloaded perceptual environments? What makes some things that seem to us to "hang together" as a meaningful sequence or cause and effect or whole "stand out" for selection in some other way? Are those meaningful wholes actually "out there in the world," or are they purely constructions on our part, subjective assumptions unmoored from the constraints of reality (which is then what, if we cannot know it absolutely or finally)? To understand Gestalt's early investigation into questions of what enables us to construct our situational understanding in one way rather than another, we need to turn to the second generation of Gestalt psychology work, in particular, the work of the most significant Gestalt psychologist of them all, Kurt Lewin.

THE CONTRIBUTIONS OF KURT LEWIN: FROM PSYCH LAB TO "LIFESPACE"

The Gestalt psychologist Kurt Lewin (1890–1947) is recognized today as the leading founder of social psychology as a discipline, group dynamics as a field of study and practice, organizational psychology, and the methodology known as *action research*, which is in wide use today in organizational studies around the world as a tool for understanding the hidden dynamics of large social systems or fields (Marrow, 1969; see also Wheeler, 1991, 2000). Lewin's contribution and legacy to fields ranging from clinical to coaching, group, and organizational settings was to take the basic pioneering work of the first generation of Gestalt research and apply it to more lifelike, real-world situations. Using the basic Gestalt picture of an active, selective subject, coconstructing, interpreting, and making meaning in the act of perception, Lewin then applied this fundamental model to new research situations in which the human subjects, instead of being in a static, values-free lab situation, were in more lifelike situations with more real stakes and real consequences of their actions.

This way of thinking about perception and behavior, integrating the early Gestalt work with real, dynamic situations, is outlined in Lewin's first academic paper, "War Landscape" (1918), sketched out while he was still a young graduate student on active duty on the German front during World War I. His thinking unfolded at this early point, growing out of the situation and concerns he saw and felt around him: Imagine a traveler moving through a valley in a war zone, Lewin wrote—like any perceiving individual, the traveler will note certain features of the environment, necessarily ignoring or deleting others and integrating the ones he or she does note into some coherent picture, for memory, comparison, orientation, meaning making, and so forth (i.e., meaning making in the sense of assigning some meaning to the perception, often in a predictive, "what's-likely-next" sense). As Gestalt research had shown over the decade before, the subject/traveler's behavior will then be based in some way on that interpreted whole picture and not simply on "everything that's there," much less on just the specific physical inputs of light and sound and so forth coming from the concrete objects in the scene.

This is basic Gestalt psychology as we have reviewed it here, although applied to a much more complex and urgent "scene" than the early work in a lab setting. Lewin's next step closely followed this same line of analysis. Each person crossing this scene, he reflected, will necessarily see a somewhat different whole picture: his or her own uniquely subjective, interpretive synthesis of the complex elements in the environment—one of them registering the farmhouse, another the church, another the color of the barn or the state of the fields or something else entirely. We even know quite a bit about particular physical characteristics of the objects and images and patterns in the scene—contrast, boundary, brightness, contiguity, and so forth (the Gestalt perceptual laws outlined previously)—that are the environmental contribution, we might say, to the whole gestalts being synthesized in the minds of the various observers.

But what about the subjective side of the construction of these whole forms, or gestalts? What is it exactly that often makes one person's interpretive synthesis of "what's there" so different from another person's perception and memory of the same scene? This is where Lewin had his next, most fertile insight, one that would open up the next level of Gestalt theory and research, leading in the decades ahead to the articulation of Gestalt therapy. Imagine one of the people crossing this valley: a soldier or scout (lost, fleeing, or maybe deserting), a local farmer, or even a lover on the way to a rendezvous. What codetermines what each of them will see (in the sense of selecting, integrating, and interpreting into usable, memorable organized pictures that he or she can further integrate with other images and learning)?

Lewin's answer was that in each case it is necessarily the need or concern that is uppermost in the individual's mind at the time that will tend to carry the most weight in selecting and organizing the perceptions of that person. The spire of the church may be a heartening symbol to one person but a potential sniper post to another and completely missing in the subsequent memory of another who was only interested, say, in finding food. A haystack might be a resource to one, a menace to the other, a refuge or an opportunity to yet another, and so on. In a real sense, each of them is operating in a quite different world, not because there is no reality that constrains and informs our interpreted pictures of it but simply because—once again—we cannot take it all in and make all of it the basis of our behavior. Our flexible and creative human perceptual equipment is inherently predisposed to organize our relevant field of awareness (Lewin, 1936), including a changing physical environment as well as a social environment of other human beings, each of them actively interpreting our shared situation in relation to her or his own agenda. Our behavior then is based on that unique creative synthesis of dynamic subjective and objective factors. We are acting and reacting, in other words, not to the real scene but in terms of the relevant, constructed, and evaluated scene synthesized in our own minds. It is this interpreted scene we respond to and behave in relation to, always with some implicit need or goal that is organizing our response.

This process of selecting, resolving, interpreting, and integrating these most relevant features into a coherent, usable whole understanding as a basis for behavior (which is, again, basic lab Gestalt, applied here to living situations), Lewin (1936) simply called *mapping*. We enter a new situation, perceive the situation by Gestalt principles in relation to our felt needs at the time, and then use that gestalt picture as a map for orienting our behavior in relation to that situation, those interpreted perceptions, and those needs (both aware and unaware). The relevant field we are mapping Lewin termed the *lifespace*, meaning the part of everything that is psychologically relevant to our own concerns as we move proactively to resolve a workable map in relation to those concerns, our awareness of our own inner states and needs, and our current and larger aims.

This naturalistic description of how our human process works (and has to work) was what the Gestaltists were looking for from the beginning: a new model based on an understanding of perception, cognition, and behavior that would emerge from the research data, rather than being imposed on the data ahead of time in the way of the older associationist (and also of the then-new Freudian libido theory, which the Gestaltists regarded as circular in that it first just asserted that all behavior was a function of one or two basic drives and then interpreted the behavior according to that assertion, without any independent research step; see

Wheeler, 2004). If many of Lewin's principles strike us today as familiar, even obvious, that of course is because along with the basic lab Gestalt principles he was starting from, these general ideas about pattern seeking and mental mapping and the crucial role of affect and emotion in cognition, behavior, and memory have permeated all of cognitive psychology, cognitive behavior psychology, psychotherapy, and beyond, so that we easily view our world today through Lewinian lenses (see Ullman, 2005).

Before leaving Lewin, we note one more area in which he was far ahead of his time: his move to treat values as part of the felt needs, aims, and desires that organize an individual's "map" for behaving in a given situation (Marrow, 1969). By interpreting values as a kind of enduring dynamic element in the individual's felt needs, Lewin recast the subject as a viable topic of research and theory in mainstream psychology, a move that would pay off with a burst of research beginning in the 1960s. Before then, the importance of the individual's system of values was a prominent new feature of Gestalt therapy building on these features of his work (see Lewin, 1936).

"The need organizes the field" (Marrow, 1969, p. 167) is how Lewin summed up much of his own work up to this point, meaning simply that the world one knows—the world one is trying to cope with and thrive in as best as possible—is the world one constructs in relation to the most urgent needs of the moment as they are felt and understood (again, including one's own needs for commitments and consistency of values, however they are felt and understood). With this formulation, Lewin related the world of interpreted perceptions, the world of inner experience, and the world of emotions and values, intentions and goals, all in one conceptual dynamic. With this framework, it became imaginable at least to apply Gestalt theory in a coherent way both to social systems such as groups and organizations (as Lewin would spend the rest of his life doing) and to the kinds of subjective personal issues and developmental dynamics psychotherapy is most often dealing with (as Gestalt psychology founders had actually thought about and suggested, without proposing any methodology for such applications; e.g., see Koehler, 1947; Koffka, 1924; Wertheimer, 1945; see also Goldstein, 1940).

How would one reveal and understand complex dynamics such as these, which after all, like all the dynamics Gestalt had theorized about and researched, are not easily visible to the naked eye? Lewin's answer—at least at the level of groups and other social systems—was in the same spirit as the whole first generation of Gestalt research he had come out of: One could challenge the "subject" (individual or larger system) with some task or problem and then look at the whole person's (or whole system's) behavioral—and now emotional as well—response to see whether hypotheses about hidden dynamics are confirmed or contradicted. This is the action research model Lewin pioneered for the study of social systems, in which no single person would have a final, authoritative perspective on the dynamics of the system as a whole. It was only a short step to apply the same approach to the complex and often hidden dynamics of an individual or a family, as in a clinical setting.

Lewin was not a clinician and did not take this step. He spent the last decade of his life, the years of World War II and immediately after, pioneering those social applications touched on previously: group dynamics, organizational studies, as well as this action research method for studying dynamics by intervening, observing, and discussing with the subjects the results of studies (Marrow, 1969). In the process he founded the Group Dynamics Lab at the Massachusetts Institute of Technology in Cambridge, Massachusetts, where his group would create the innovative "t-groups," out of which the sensitivity training and encounter groups of the 1960s and 1970s would emerge. He also founded the National Training Labs, for many decades the pioneering center in the world for applied group dynamics and organizational consultant training (Marrow, 1969).

Thus, it remained for an unlikely pair of psychoanalytic critics and writers, both of them reinventing themselves in midcareer in the immediate postwar years, to see the potential for a radically new approach to psychotherapy in the Gestalt psychology model as it had evolved in the hands of Lewin and others of academic Gestalt's second generation (e.g., Goldstein, 1939). In Chapter 3 we turn to the theory they articulated (Perls, Hefferline, & Goodman, 1951) and the methodology that grew out of it, but to understand better how the Gestalt therapy model arose as it did, we complete the history and roots of the model by sketching out briefly the climate in which this new theory and method would emerge, together with the background of influences, deep concerns, and creative innovations both men would bring to their remarkable project.

GOODMAN AND PERLS: THE BIRTH OF GESTALT THERAPY

The postwar years of the mid-20th century were an extremely fertile time in the evolution of psychotherapy and its related fields. The war years had left unimaginable suffering, desolation, and loss in their wake, but the crisis and collapse of so many "isms" and absolute ideologies that had held much of Europe and other cultures in sway across the first half of the century also meant that rigid and absolute authority was now often viewed with suspicion in the aftermath of so much societal upheaval in fields ranging from politics to culture to religion and more. Greater faith in the independent judgment and ethical core of the autonomous individual was the new order of the day.

It was in this climate that social theorist and cultural critic Paul Goodman and renegade psychoanalyst Fritz Perls met and partnered on a wholly new theory project for a new psychotherapy model (along with Laura Perls, who took a training role essential to development of their ideas; see Stoehr, 1994b). Their project would be nothing less than an entirely new approach, based on Gestalt psychology and closely related sources, to understanding human behavior, perception and meaning making, relationship and values, health and dysfunction—a radically new theory and method for psychotherapy based on Gestalt-derived ideas. Their starting point was a now-lost, unfinished monograph that Perls had brought with him from South Africa, where he and his wife had spent over a decade in wartime exile, practicing and developing their first book and considering ideas for the next. In this first work, *Ego Hunger and Aggression: A Critique of Freud's Theory and Method* (1947), coauthored with Laura Perls but published under Fritz Perls's name alone (Wysong & Rosenfeld, 1982), the Perlses had articulated their theory of oral aggression, one that Fritz had tried and failed to present to Freud before the war (Stoehr, 1994b).

It is not clear in retrospect whether Perls realized at first the full potential of the material this new monograph was presenting, which would take the two authors and their new model far beyond a critique of Freud's legacy into a wholly new understanding of human pathology and optimal health and of the role and operating principles, at least, of therapy in supporting movement from one to the other. Goodman saw immediately the potential in Perls's thinking for a radically new articulation of self theory and human relations; his role in the project quickly progressed from editor to coauthor to lead author of the second theoretical volume, *Novelty, Excitement, and Growth,* of the two-part series that would be released as *Gestalt Therapy: Excitement and Growth in the Human Personality* (Goodman, 1951; see also Stoehr, 1994b).

Although there were important differences in the two authors' sources, backgrounds, interests, and agendas, they were joined in their open debt to the profound legacy of Freud, while still sharing a deep concern that the classical Freudian model leaned far too heavily on the idea of adjustment to society at the expense of individual creativity, self-exploration and self-expression, desire and passion, authentic relationship, and social reform. In the postwar climate of consumerism, mass industrialization, and rigid anticommunism, they saw the danger that psychotherapy in its classical analytic form could become a tool for conformism and social passivity (Stoehr, 1994b). Their vision, by contrast, was that by drawing on the legacy of Gestalt psychology, they could combine the radical insights of Freud (and especially the Freudian revisionist Wilhelm Reich, 1945) with the more action-oriented psychology of Kurt Lewin to create a model in which psychotherapy would reclaim its place as a primary agent for human freedom, social progressivism, and a new capacity for deeper passion, satisfaction, and meaning in living. To see how they proposed this would work, we turn to their new theory in Chapter 3.

3

Theory

A t the conceptual and methodological center of their radical new therapy
model, Gestalt therapy, Paul Goodman and Fritz and Laura Perls placed
the integrative concept of *contact* (Perls, Hefferline, & Goodman, 1951). This
term captured and summarized the central findings of Gestalt psychology:
We make sense of and deal with our world not by passively receiving (and
adjusting to) some exact objective reality but by using an active process of
reaching out, selecting, interpreting, and organizing whole pictures of our
situations and then basing some behavior or some action on that interpreted picture. This most often happens fairly automatically in a single
integrated act of perception, interpretation, and action without reflective,
conscious awareness—or we may stop and be more aware of trying to "figure
out what's going on," strategize, evaluate, and make conscious choices. Either
way, the process has the same structure: We approach situations with some
need (or a number of needs), both in conscious awareness and without full

http://dx.doi.org/10.1037/14527-003
Gestalt Therapy, by G. Wheeler and L. Axelsson

awareness of our experience and needs. We then understand the situation and take actions in relation to those perceptions and subjective needs.

Each person does this in both unique and partly routine ways, depending on her or his history, culture, values, conditioning, and experiences and also on his or her desires, needs, values, creative capacities, and perceptions of the situation, short and longer term. Responses and behaviors are ideally partly patterned and habitual and partly ad hoc, or creatively responsive to the situation (in relation to the individual's goals and needs at the time); too much patterning and repetition in responding results in a rigid or unspontaneous gestalt formation, which is always the same no matter how much the situation varies. Too much spontaneity (too little basic patterning or context) means a chaotic experience and chaotic behavior. True creativity is a "sweet spot" blending and integrating the two poles: conservation (of past experience) and spontaneity (the new response to the unique situation).

That's how human behavior is dynamically organized, Goodman and Perls argued—in more or less effective ways to cope with the situations in which we find ourselves. In different areas and situations our experience and behavior may be more or less freely responsive and creative or more rigidly patterned and, in this sense, unfree. Here they agreed with Freud (1933/1965) that neurosis is unfree repetition, a mere reaction rather than a response in the full creative sense. This is contact (experience plus behavior), whether creatively free or neurotically unfree. The therapy is then the analysis of contact in this sense. But by *analysis*, Goodman and Perls pictured something quite different from classical Freudian or psychodynamically informed models. Their analysis was more dialogic and relational, more action based and experimental, and more concerned with the client's constructive process of interpreting, valuing, goal setting, and meaning making. The following are the broad areas in which the new Gestalt-based perspective and model differed from models that were current at the time.

THE ROLE OF THE PATIENT OR CLIENT

In place of the more passive Freudian patient, meekly "swallowing" (as they saw it) or reactively defending against the authoritative interpretations of the analyst (only to have each defense analyzed until the patient agreed to the imposed interpretation), Goodman and Perls had something much more mutually active in mind: Therapy should be a place where the client could at last stop swallowing society's or other people's values and rules and begin challenging them in an active quest based on his or her desires, emotions, and value preferences; on experimentation with new strategies; and on a deeper knowledge and expression of his or her authentic creative self.

THE ROLE OF THE THERAPIST

This changes the position of the analyst/therapist from that of a detached or neutral expert pronouncing judgment on the client's behavior and understanding, to a participant/observer, a fully engaged partner in the therapeutic process. The therapist challenges the client's behavior and experience and understanding not from a position of expert correction but rather in the service of restoring the client's healthy process of constructing, revising, discarding, and recreating "wholes" of understanding and behavior (because from a Gestalt perspective, behavior will always be in response to one's interpreted understanding of the situation at the time; the two things cannot be separated).

Thus, it is the client's experience that is prioritized, not the therapist's authority. The therapist's skills and expertise remain crucial, but that expertise consists not in providing the right answers to the meaning of the client's experience but in facilitating a particular type of encounter in which the client discovers and creates those meanings for him- or herself in a collaborative process of contact, in the sense outlined earlier. The therapist's expertise then rests on her or his capacity for authenticity in contact and relationship, not for the sake of the therapist's self-expression but in support of the client's quest for greater understanding and deeper, more flexible contact capacities. In the process, the therapist often urges the client to slow down, relax unexamined and fear-based patterns of rigidity, and notice features of his or her process, pointing out contradictions as the therapist experiences them (between affect and content, for example, or observations/events and interpretations/conclusions drawn from it by the client) and offering challenges to the client's understanding, especially in areas in which the client is reporting dissatisfaction, dysfunction, or distress.

Some of this may sound similar to cognitive behavior therapy models (e.g., see Young, 1999), but Perls and Goodman recognized (as contemporary cognitive behavior therapy writers often do as well) that verbal and analytic accounts of our experience are far from the full picture: Our *gestalts of understanding*—our interpretations of experience and the world—are naturally subject to the same selective biases or out-of-awareness distortions that support old, rigid, and out-of-awareness behavior patterns that are the source of the problem in the first place. This is what the Gestalt psychology model is all about.

Specifically, with their agenda of greater personal freedom in a freer society, Goodman and Perls shared the concern that these learned, often rigid understandings may not be authentic and autonomous at all but imposed on us from outside forces, whether through early conditioning or by the pressure of social conformism. That is, they may be social *introjects*, a kind of conformity to parental or societal messages and norms, an idea that they viewed as the blind spot of the classic Freudian adjustment model they hoped to get away from. Thus, they brought a whole series of new conceptual tools to bear on challenging rigid received beliefs and fears, all drawn from a more holistic, Gestalt-based understanding of how we construct our experience.

These new techniques and tools included first (a) a new understanding and use of the therapeutic relationship, yielding a new sense of therapeutic dialogue; then (b) a deeper use of affect and emotion; (c) a new level of attention to the body; and finally, (d) the use of experiment in therapy. Each of these became a major theme and tool in supporting the client to deconstruct those tightly integrated behaviors and understanding, moving the therapeutic encounter beyond merely talking about an issue (Perls, 1969) to directly experiencing it in the present moment and situation, moving toward a new capacity for a more creative, open-ended, and less rule-bound approach to living. A later parallel to this Gestalt psychology idea of a tightly integrated "whole" of action, interpretation, emotion, and belief is schema theory in cognitive behavior therapy (Young,

1999). In this sense a *schema* is essentially a gestalt of understanding and emotion plus embodiment and behavior.

THE THERAPEUTIC RELATIONSHIP

By shifting to greater equality and a participant/observer dynamic in the therapeutic relationship (in place of detached expert and more passive patient), the new therapy opened the way to a different and much freer use of the therapist's experience in therapy—in sharp contrast to the detached, neutral traditional Freudian analyst of the day. Following Lewin, we can understand that any relationship at any given moment is a situation in which *both* people make interpretations of the conditions as they subjectively experience them. By making more of his or her experience transparent, the therapist makes the coconstructed relational situation much more available as material for the client to process with more awareness. In this way the therapeutic relationship becomes a living lab for the same issues the client is likely dealing with in other relationships and other situations of life. This then enables the transfer of skills and insights experienced in therapy to other less protected and thus more challenging situations in "real life" (i.e., life outside the protection and special support of the therapy situation).

Using his or her experience in the therapeutic encounter is not a matter of "anything goes" for the therapist: The session is still in the service of the client, and the therapist remains thoughtful about when and what to share and what not to share. Therapist *authenticity* never means sharing things that are not relevant to the client's goals and issues; rather, it most often means noticing when an issue or difficulty in the client's life is being enacted in the therapeutic relationship and then opening that up for exploration (as opposed to interpreting it as being about some other relationship, most often with a parent, as would have been a standard analytic practice of the times). To make use of the client–therapist relationship in the therapy process, the therapist has to be fully aware of his or her own experience and, when it supports the client's growth of understanding and contact capacity, share parts of that experience with the client.

For example, if a client were to take a position of always rejecting, interrupting, or contradicting any perspective or challenge the therapist offers, the Gestalt therapist would not respond, "I'm getting really annoyed by all these contradictions" (which may well only replicate the response the client often gets to this behavior in daily life), nor would he or she say (in a caricature of the traditional interpretive analyst), "Now you're treating me as if I were your corrective, punitive mother—and at the same time you're identifying with her aggression, by constantly correcting me." This kind of analytic interpretation, Goodman and Perls felt, might have some validity at times, yet stating it out loud would likely only reinforce the client's contact pattern of compliance (or reactivity) to authority rather than build a capacity for more complex, thoughtful contact that would transfer to other relationships and situations outside the therapy hour.

Instead of interpreting, the therapist might say, "I'm feeling frustrated now because I want to be here in a way that is potentially helpful, and if you only tell me you disagree with what I say, I don't learn much about what you think and feel. It leaves me to figure out on my own by trial and error what you mean and what might be helpful to you." This kind of sharing can readily become the basis for an experiment—for example, "What would it be like if every time I offer some observation or perspective, you were to tell me first what part of that makes sense to you and then what part you disagree with? We could do this just as an experiment to see what feelings and thoughts come up. Otherwise the moment goes by so fast that we don't get to find out more about each feeling that might be involved." In this way the therapist is being true to her or his experience but not just for its own sake; rather, this kind of self-report places more information (the reaction of the other person) at the service of the client, opening up new possibilities rather than closing the door in the face of the client's problematic contact. (For further discussion of experiment as a concept and as a method, see the section "Action and Experimentation as Therapeutic Tools" later in this chapter.)

The art and discipline here is to exemplify and model the practice of reporting emotional self-experience and not make interpretive analyses or impositions, both for the reasons outlined previously and because the client is likely to be inexperienced in sensing, owning, and expressing authentic present emotional experience (and in having it received with interest and inquiry, not interpretation or other corrective counterinput). This capacity for emotional self-contact is key to greater autonomy and authenticity and more complex, satisfying relational contact, which are among the chief aims of Gestalt therapy. If the therapist is concerned about burdening the client with knowledge of the therapist's experience, the Gestalt solution is to bring attention to that topic—the present relationship at the present moment—in the live relational "lab" that is therapy.

experiment

THE FOCUS ON EMOTIONAL EXPERIENCE

A second tool for unlocking and opening up the client's contact process is to slow down and simply focus longer and with greater intensity and support on the feelings that come up when not engaging in habitual behavior or "contact style" (Wheeler, 1991). The immediate goal, after all, is to support the client in opening up areas that are too rigidly integrated into pre-constructed whole sequences of thought, emotion, and behavior, blocking open experimentation and new learning in that area of living. If the therapist quickly moves to offer an explanation for everything that comes up, it would only serve, Goodman and Perls felt, to leave the client's habitual contact patterns in place. The therapy could then quickly become only a discussion about the issues, missing the opportunity to come to grips· with them directly with the "charge" of the real situation and relationship in the present moment—all the emotions, assumptions, and unaware behaviors that are being compressed (and lost for exploration) into the habitual response pattern in the first place—hence the frequent Gestalt therapy exhortation "Just stay with that feeling, breathe into it, and let's see together where it leads," moving into the structure of the present moment rather than away from it into what probably is a safer, more distanced discussion of a kind the client has likely already had, perhaps again and again.

In this way the therapist opens up the dynamic roots of an unsatisfying behavior in the present situation, where it is actually being lived out "here and now." This is what it means to treat the therapeutic situation as an authentic relationship in its own right rather than as something just transferred from other, earlier relationships. If, as in the earlier example, the client has a basic contact habit or "move," such as indiscriminately contradicting and rejecting most or all input, at least in situations where a perceived, felt power difference may be present, that gestalt pattern, that whole of behavior and understanding, was constructed originally to manage some perceived threat in the past. When the felt threat and the response strategy have passed out of awareness, the whole original sequence of per-ceived approach, apprehension or interpretation of danger, feelings of fear, chronic defensive or distancing response of contradicting or rebuffing the approach, and the lessening of the fear becomes an integrated behavioral pattern, more or less automated and more or less extreme depending on the present triggers and the present perceived conditions of safety or threat.

What good will it likely do, Goodman and Perls asked, to interpret that, offering the therapist's guess about the client's out-of-awareness experi-ence, which would then only likely be experienced as one more instance of a threatening approach, one more possible menace or imposition to be managed? How much richer and more productive it can be in therapy, they argued, to join the client in just "being with" that moment, letting the feelings arise, and begin to open up that automated (and now buried or invisible) sequence, letting the client first experience all the dynamic parts that are going into that pattern and then making her or his own interpre-tation about where it comes from and how it might be put back together differently. As we will see later, the other available tools—body experience and experiment—further support and deepen this in the context of the relationship of therapeutic partnership, which is more equal and authen-tic in these ways.

The therapeutic situation and relationship could best be character-ized, Goodman (1951) proposed, as a *safe emergency*, the basic Gestalt therapy idea of restoring a dynamic, flexible balance between safe habits and creative new moves (which by definition are often more exposed and vulnerable, at least at first). The therapy aims to be *safe*, through the attuned relationship based on nonjudgmental, nonauthoritarian, non-corrective respect for the client's experience and meaning making, and also an *emergency*, as a result of the new, modulated amount of risk that is still under relational conditions creating enough safety to support that new experiment.

THE FOCUS ON EMBODIMENT

In addition to slowing down to focus on out-of-awareness feelings, Goodman and Perls also made rich use of the work of one of Freud's most creative, revisionist followers, the psychoanalyst Wilhelm Reich. Reich's insight was that past emotional and relational conflicts that are buried (or *integrated* and *habituated*, in Gestalt psychology terms) are still carried in the present by the client, not just in buried emotions but also in "frozen" or habituated bodily tensions. Thus, attention to the body constitutes the third major focus of Gestalt therapy, in the context of this new kind of therapeutic relationship, supplementing the use of attention to feelings and emotions in the process of slowing down and deconstructing the too tightly structured patterns of behavior and understanding that the Gestalt model holds as often lying behind the client's current difficulties.

One of the main techniques in using this tool is support for slowing down, noticing, and pointing out body tensions or habits (especially ones that contradict the client's verbal sharing or self-awareness) and staying with those states till a new possibility, a new tension, or new experiment emerges. For example, the therapist might say, "You're telling me something terribly sad (or angry or embarrassing, etc.), yet you have a big smile (or a clenched fist or perhaps a frozen jaw; perhaps the client's breathing has stopped or the voice has become small, and so on). What would happen if we stop and you just stay with that smile (or fist or jaw or breathing)?" Tears can be the first result of this kind of supported pause in an automated contact sequence; the buried frustration and pain of carrying the underlying issue and feelings so long and so alone come to the surface.

This may then lead into the kind of dialogue or *empty-chair work* Gestalt therapy is often known for, which entails the client shifting from one chair or stance to another to give voice to the person or message imagined as the source of that particular message. Thus, the client can experience an unintegrated point of view within him- or herself directly and often resolve it. For example, the therapist might propose, "What would your smile (or fist or breath-holding) be saying to us, if it had its own voice?" The client might respond, "My smile says, 'I can take this, I can't let this get me down' or 'I mustn't let you see how sad I'm really feeling . . . don't let the world really see you.'" The habituated or stuck contact pattern begins to open to the possibility of a new, more open-ended response pattern to similar situations and feelings.

AWARENESS, CONSCIOUSNESS, AND THE UNCONSCIOUS

In Gestalt therapy, the comprehensive term *awareness* refers, as in Gestalt psychology, to all those selected features of our situation (internal as well as external) that we register, integrate, and respond to in some way, with and/or without consciousness. These selected features include everything we have attended to in the earlier discussion—thoughts, emotions, and body states, as well as aspects of our physical and social or relational situation, both in and out of consciousness—interpreted and integrated in relation to our background of memories, beliefs, assumptions, needs, and perceptions of what we need to manage now and in the future. This is the integrated background out of which our behavior emerges at any present moment; it is how our organizing process works, enabling us to deal with ever-changing situations in relation to our ongoing and ever-changing needs. Thus, the term *awareness* includes both conscious and unconscious domains; the Gestalt model does not view these two domains as sharply or rigidly distinct, as in the classical Freudian model. To be sure, most of our behavior is the integrated result of processes that are outside our aware-ness, but the right balance of attentional focus and fuller awareness plus relational support can bring the out-of-awareness dynamics back into the present contact, where they can then be open to new and different patterns of integration.

Awareness may often be divided loosely into conscious awareness, body awareness, emotional awareness, and so forth, and then extended to include awareness of the other person and of the conditions of the field or situation (to which we are always responding, with or without conscious awareness). Awareness is a basic tool in Gestalt that is used with each of these techniques and interventions by calling attention and focus (supported by the self-support of more open breathing plus the other support of the therapist's attuned presence) to feeling states, the body, or the present dialogic relational situation. Thus, in Gestalt the therapist frequently asks questions such as, "What's it like for you now when . . . ?" or "What comes up for you when . . . ?" or "What do you feel when I point that out?" All of these are questions about experience in the present moment and situation (again, not with the aim of changing or correcting that experience but to open up the dynamics of the present contact, with an aim of opening new possibilities for patterns of integration and flexibility).

The present relationship and dialogue can be called into awareness, for example, by asking, "What's it like for you right now when I tell you I'm experiencing you in this (or that) way?" or "What's it like to share that feeling with me now and have me see you in this way?" or even, "What's it like for you here and now, as we sit here together? How safe does it feel here? Do you feel like I'm getting you in a way you can feel? What's that like? When do you feel less safe—or too exposed—here with me now?" In this way the relationship becomes a lab for exploration and experimentation in all the ways discussed earlier, using focused awareness as the main technique.

ACTION AND EXPERIMENTATION AS THERAPEUTIC TOOLS

We have already seen how the focus on awareness in Gestalt naturally passes into some imagined or emergent experiment. This is in sharp contrast to the classical psychodynamic practice of the day, when the analytic interpretation was seen as designed to block *enactment* (which by definition would just be a neurotic repetition of a defense in the face of pressure or conflict). *Experiment,* by contrast, is understood in the sense of Lewin's action research discussed in Chapter 2. That is, the purpose of an experiment is not so much to learn or practice some new skill, much less to "fix" anything (though all those things may also happen in the process of experimenting); rather, the aim is to bring to the surface underlying dynamics, which are out of awareness and out of sight of both client and therapist (though the therapist may have some good hypotheses of what the underlying issues are). In other words, the goal is always learning— slowing down and deepening experience in the service of new under-standing and new possibilities for more flexible and effective response.

Experiments in therapy may be formal and planned or informal and spontaneous; Goodman and Perls gave us examples of both kinds. Either way, they center on the present situation, with present emotions and pres-ent felt needs and goals, and always with the aim of a deeper understand-ing of how we are constructing our contact process and where that might become open to new creative adaptation.

A more formal experiment is the classic Gestalt *two-chair work* (a vari-ation of the classic Gestalt empty-chair work described earlier), in which the client, faced with a dilemma, conflict, or choice, outlines some polar positions or conflicting voices about the situation and then actually sits in each chair, embodying just that particular voice and point of view. An example is the familiar situation of conflicting desires or a desire in conflict with a cautionary voice, correcting or warning about safety and exposure to risk. On the one hand, for example, the client may want to tell her or his boss (or parent or spouse or other important person) where and why she or he needs more appreciation, more money, or more freedom to develop a project, to drop a too-burdensome, unfair role or responsibility, or to have better treatment in some other way; on the other hand, a paralyzing cloud of apprehension and anxiety may lead to thinking, "Don't do it. Don't risk it. Don't provoke the negative consequences that will follow," more loudly and sternly the closer the client comes to taking the prohibited step. This is a familiar kind of issue in therapy: a desire (a self-assertion, a creative idea, an unexpressed resentment) in conflict with a set of fears (e.g., people will not like you, you will be punished, you will lose the marginal acceptance you have now—the kinds of feelings that can lead to even harder-to-contact depths of guilt, shame, and doubt about self-worth).

The client can give fuller voice to each of these positions in turn—the desire, the warning voice, the feelings and longings and fears behind each of them—and there can be dialogue back and forth between the positions, all still in the voice of the client, who may move back and forth between the chairs. The client may often be able to identify the sources of the voices (e.g., "That's my grandmother's voice, most of all, telling me I can do it, that I'm special and wonderful and can have all those things" or "That stern voice is my father, always telling me not to stick my neck out, not to take a risk"). By spending more time within the voices, the client might also be surprised to discover, for example, that the father's voice is more afraid than judging, more protective than punitive.

The same kind of experimental enactment may happen more organically and dialogically, using the "relational lab" of the therapy situation more directly. In the earlier example, the client was asked what it might be like if before each critical, dismissing, or distancing response (to whatever the therapist offered), he or she first agreed to offer some positive response to some part of what the therapist said that he or she could agree with. What would happen to the distance between the client and the therapist? What would it be like for the client? Would it be greater or less? Either way, would it be a good thing or a "bad" thing (in the sense of being less safe and more problematic) or some more complex mixture in between? Using this more naturalistic experiment of enacting the repeating contact habit in the real therapeutic relationship, client and therapist alike get to know much more about what this contact style (which may be causing problems in the client's life and relationships) is actually serving. By doing the opposite of some too-typical behavior pattern or response, the feelings that the habitual pattern was containing and mitigating are clearer.

An alternative, when this kind of direct deconstruction is not working, is to propose the parallel experiment of simply doing the behavior more—in this case, for example, intentionally taking pains to always contradict or correct each thing the therapist says. This can "loosen up" out-of-touch feelings and thoughts as the exaggerated behavior becomes freeing or burdensome or perhaps comic, embarrassing, or even sad, as the loneliness of it is contacted more deeply. This is analogously like trying to relax a habitually tense muscle: Because the underlying emotional tension has likely become habituated, it can be difficult to find the "off button" for the muscle constriction, which has long since become automated and lost to awareness. What can be done is to tighten it more, enabling us to find or become aware of that muscular–nervous connection and allowing us to experiment more easily with relaxing it.

In Gestalt therapy work, this kind of move has become known as a *paradoxical approach to change:* Perform the targeted sequence or movement more, not less, and many of the same feelings, beliefs, and memories that are tied up in that habituated pattern will often come into awareness and be available for change. Here we see the influence of Reich's work on *character armor,* the holding of old neurotic conflicts as patterns of embodied tension that can be loosened directly to open up hidden feelings (Reich, 1945, mentioned earlier as one of Goodman and Perls's chief neo-Freudian influences). This kind of therapeutic maneuver of emphasis and exaggeration has also been termed the *paradoxical theory of change* (Beisser, 1970) and is often referenced that way in Gestalt discussions (perhaps somewhat confusingly, because the move is not a theory *per se,* so much as a technique for supporting attention in the service of basic Gestalt exploration and deconstruction of all those kinds of tightly integrated sequences of perception, interpretation, and behavior we discuss here). We return to the topic of a fuller Gestalt theory of change in the discussion of contemporary Gestalt therapy practice later in the chapter.

As experiments and explorations such as these open up new possibilities, the client may also find that an old underlying and self-organizing dynamic of right and wrong, approval and shame, surfaces and begins to soften. As this develops, the therapist continues to make use of relational connectedness, emotional resonance, attention to embodiment, new connections, and meaning making, all in the context of a therapeutic relationship dedicated to the client's goals, values, and expanding contact range. (We say more about the particular Gestalt approach to the experience and dynamics of shame later in the chapter.)

Here the basic Lewinian insight about perception as problem solving opens up the larger idea that experiment in Gestalt is not just a technique or method but an attitude or an approach to life at a larger level. This stance underlies and transcends the therapy setting, amounting to a kind of living philosophy of life as an ongoing process of experiment, learning, and ever-growing capacity for ever-more complex creative contact and relationship. Everything we experience, everything we do, can be looked at as experiment, part of a lifelong series of learning exercises that build on, challenge, confirm, deepen, and at times transform our integrated "ground" of past experiences and our evolving capacity for complex experience. Our understanding and our perceptions are always interpretive, never final; our growth in contact capacities—for deeper meanings, more complex contacting, and greater effectiveness and satisfaction—can be lifelong. The shift to an experimental stance on living and learning is support for these transformational processes, both in therapy and all through life.

THE GOALS OF THERAPY AND THE IDEAL OF HEALTH

One of Goodman and Perls's shared concerns was the idea that Freudian analysis placed far too heavy an emphasis on a conservative goal of adjustment, which they saw as inevitably leading to social conformism, the dulling of passion and creativity, and passivity in political and community life. In its place they held up a different goal: creative adjustment, which they took as synonymous with healthy growth. In the Gestalt therapy model our basic human nature is lifelong *growth*, which can be defined as the capacity to integrate ever-increasing complexity of response and meaning making in relationship with our world. We have the capacity to meet evermore complex challenges creatively and sustainably, with new experiences and new forms that remain rooted in a web of connection and communication.

When asked for a definition of mental health, Freud famously answered tersely, "Love and work." A fuller Gestalt answer might be "capacity for love, work, and play"; the capacity to allow for the free play of experiment is central to a Gestalt psychology understanding of creativity (Wheeler, 1989, 2003). Because the model places creativity of response at the center of the goals of therapy, it would not necessarily include a single "healthy" image; healthy individuals in Gestalt differ widely from one another. What they have in common is the capacity for ongoing growth in contact capacity and relationship.

43

Rather than describing an end point, Gestalt emphasizes the living process we need and use to continue our growth through life. At the same time, we know that each person's growth and development will likely be uneven across different life situations and challenges—this is true for ourselves as well as for our clients. In one area our clients (or we ourselves) have an open creative process that meets new challenges with flexible responses based on an integrated history of previous learning, resources, and past creative responses; but in the same person in another area we may also find inhibition, rigid habituation, and a low level of resources (or use of available resources), both internal (self-supports, such as skills base and past experience) and external ("other" supports, the capacity to draw on available support from others). These are the issues and topics our clients (or we ourselves) bring into therapy in the face of different challenges at different times of life. Gestalt therapy, as Goodman and Perls outlined it, moves to meet these challenges with the tools and concepts outlined here, always supporting and restoring a natural arc of contact based on greater awareness, greater response repertoire, and ongoing learning and growth where these were undeveloped or interrupted.

PRESENT-CENTERED WORK AND THE ROLE OF HISTORY

Lewin emphasized that a problem or an issue that occurs in the present must be the result of dynamic forces operating in the present. Phrased this way, the point seems self-evident: No matter the historical roots of an issue or problem, that original conflict or challenge in past development must be still present and active, at least potentially, blocking or freezing flexibility of response whenever that challenge presents itself again. Goodman and Perls, with their deep (if critical) appreciation of Freud, did not reject or neglect the importance of history and development. Rather, the authors felt that if the therapist takes history and childhood as the entry points into the issue, the likely outcome will be just discussion about the issues—which is potentially endless—with little opportunity to experience, relax, open up, and thus deconstruct the stuck and problematic response habit, which would otherwise have led to a new synthesis and a deeper, more

44

flexible contact. The Freudian patient is one who risks "understanding everything and changing nothing," Goodman is reported to have quipped (E. Nevis, personal communication, July 18, 1976). By starting with fuller presence and contact—first by the therapist her- or himself, and then through the tools and techniques outlined earlier for enriching self-awareness, emotional presence, embodied awareness, and experimental "play"—the therapist aims to support an experience in which the client may try out a new behavior, potentially leading to new meaning-making and newly integrated understanding.

RESISTANCE AND THE DEFENSES

Contact, in this Gestalt sense of the ongoing flow of new experience being integrated into (and challenging or changing) our accumulating learning, can then be viewed across time as a natural, lifelong process arc of accumulating growth as well as the capacity for further growth. What happens when this natural process arc becomes interrupted, as in all the cases of outdated, stuck, or frozen gestalt formation such as we have been discussing here? What are those mechanisms of interruption, and how does knowing more about them help the therapist deal with specific instances of problems and developmental blocks in clients' lives and material? With this articulation of a new vision for psychotherapy in place, Goodman and Perls then outlined a clinical map of prototypical ways in which this natural human arc of contact and growth may typically become interrupted and chronically stuck.

Where the older psychoanalytic model had spoken of *defenses* (which were conceived of as solutions to overwhelming instinct pressures; A. Freud, 1937; S. Freud, 1933/1965), here the focus is on challenges past and present in dealing with our relational environment, including our inner world of thoughts and feelings, impulses and needs, as well as our outer world of situations and other people. Given the conditions and our resources and capacities at the time, each of us solved those challenges with the most creative solutions we could assemble and integrate. Where those conditions were too daunting, our needs too urgent, and our capacities and resources not yet developed enough for a more flexible solution, each of us

45

came up with more rigid, less open-ended solutions that may still be with us today in the form of all those rigid, nonevolving contact habits and moves that may get in our way and block new development—the kinds of issues and response patterns we as therapists see in our clients in therapy (and, of course, in ourselves at particular times and in particular areas of challenge).

Goodman and Perls identified five typical or directional moves each of us may habitually make, often old, out-of-date solutions to problems we could be addressing in new ways today, if only we could be supported in taking the old habit apart and tolerating the uncertainty of not knowing how to respond till a newer, more functional and flexible pattern or sequence can be created, practiced, and integrated.

Confluence

Normally, as they saw it, we experience a dynamic sense of a self-boundary, which both joins and distinguishes us with and from others and from our physical environment. *Confluence* is the lessening or loss of this "boundary of difference." As such, enforced confluence (i.e., where differentiation is not allowed) is at the root of maladaptive learning and contact patterns in childhood development (a particular concern of Perls's; Perls, 1947, 1969) and also at the root of social conformism and oppressive societal rules and restrictions (a central concern of Goodman's; Stoehr, 1994a).

Introjection

When confluence is chronic or extreme, we are forced to learn by *introjection*, which is the taking in or "swallowing" of ideas and positions of others without any critical stage of "chewing"—that is, reflecting, taking the input apart and breaking it down, trying out which parts fit and which parts are not authentic for us individually and socially, and then integrating those parts that are nourishing or useful and discarding or revising the rest. Clearly, both these primary contact interruptions grow out of Goodman and Perls's concern (and the concern of the times, as we discussed at the end of Chapter 2) that authentic individual judgment and choice may easily get lost in modern mass industrial society, to the detriment of both individual health and healthy societal functioning (again, a central focus of Goodman's life and work; see Stoehr, 1994b; here and in the rest of the discussion of contact interruptions, see Perls, Hefferline, & Goodman, 1951).

Projection

Projection, closely following the Freudian concept of this same term, is the act of disowning some impulse or thought or part of the self that is not acceptable or comfortable for us to own up to (A. Freud, 1937). Thus, if sexual desire, say, or anger or assertiveness (often judged negatively in women in our society, and even more so in in those times), or tenderness or vulnerability (likewise often more problematic for men in their socialization, then and now), or any other quality or behavior is held as inadmissible or shameful, the person may seek to lessen that tension by desensitizing it (as, say, with particular sexual desires or just sexual impulses in general), blanking out awareness of it (this would be James's, 1890/2007, *selective inattention*, discussed in Chapter 2 but raised here to a dysfunctional extreme), and then compensating by imagining it or an exaggerated attention to it in others.

Like Freudian and other writers (Allport, 1954), Goodman and Perls saw this interruption or resistance to contact as the underlying mechanism behind societal projection. If the society has puritanical values about sex, for example (as the society of their times certainly did, especially by today's standards), then rather than seeing oneself as bad in this way, people might see others as embodying this dangerous or immoral trait: women, say, or men (depending on who is doing the projecting), or bohemians, leftists, sexual or other minorities, foreigners, and so on. As with all resistances, this projection can be traced to harsh childrearing plus aversive and punitive social norms; at the social level the only answer would lie in progressive social reform and education, but in individual cases therapy could and should support the reowning of everything human, as Goodman put it (Stoehr, 1994a).

Retroflection

Retroflection, like all the resistances, is the interruption of a normal, organic contact process (i.e., the unfolding of a healthy desire, only blocked or distorted), in this case by turning the desire back toward the self. Psychoanalysis had long seen depression as involving a holding in of aggression, turning punishment toward the self (S. Freud, 2005). Goodman and Perls expanded on this, seeing other activities, such as self-stimulation and self-soothing, as likewise interruptions of a natural expressive reach outward.

Egotism

With each of these archetypal contact resistances, the interruption is conceived in terms of a physical state or motion; thus, retroflection is a turning inward, projecting is an expulsion outward, introjection is a suspension of normal resistance and destructuring (Perls, 1947) at the self-boundary, whereas confluence is a passive collapse of the self-boundary entirely, at least for that issue and situation. *Egotism* is then a rigidification of the boundary, an inability to let go organically in what was termed *final contact* (Goodman, 1951), holding back from the final release of arrival in a journey of contact, the final thoughtless melding of the artist with her or his materials in the act of creating, a healthy dissolution of separateness in a kind of creative union or flow.

   This is one of the places where the theoretical differences between the two authors—which were partly suspended for the brief period of their collaboration on this seminal project—still persist in the emphasis and urgency of their central concerns. Goodman, with his abiding concerns about the loss of healthy social connections (see Stoehr, 1994a), introduced this idea of a healthy loss of the self-boundary (and the contact interruption of fearing and resisting that loss, in full contact), which was not among Perls's much longer list of possible contact interruptions listed in his earlier book on oral aggression and the importance of breaking with infantile dependency in the move toward mature development (Perls, 1947). *Maturity*, wrote Perls (1969), is the move from (early) dependence to mature independence, a move that he saw as threatened by confluence and all its accompanying ills. Perls's metaphor of reference was always eating and digestion, which fit with his revision to Freud's theory and method in exploring oral aggression as a necessary and healthy drive, to break this dependency (Perls, 1947).

Goodman, for his part, most often used a sexual metaphor to illustrate his concepts. Thus "full or final contact" (Goodman, 1951, pp. 416ff) is more like orgasm than digestion, more a melting of the self into the other (or the artist into her or his work) than an aggressive "chewing" out of a concern about being dominated or invaded. We might say that Perls, like Freud, saw the relationship as something to be risked only in the context of energized self-expression (Perls, 1947; see also Wheeler, 2000), whereas Goodman saw the self as fulfilled in relationship, with the greater risk being the missed opportunity for nourishment and reenergizing if contact is constantly interrupted at the end by the resistance of egotism.

In this way Perls kept one foot always firmly planted in a Freudian register, where the crisis of development centers on the oedipal conflict, in which the growing male child breaks the dependency on the mother, internalizing the aggression of the threatening father (S. Freud, 1933/1965). Gestalt therapy, however, is squarely planted in a relational register, where the ongoing challenge of life for the subjective self is to take up a fulfilling, sustainable relationship with the environment (i.e., the social environment). As Lewin observed, the human field is a world of other human beings:

> The American cultural ideal of the self-made man, of everyone standing on his own feet, is as tragic a picture as the initiative-destroying dependence on a benevolent despot. We all need each other. This type of interdependence is the greatest challenge to the maturity of individual and group functioning. (Marrow, 1969, p. 201)

Thus, the subsequent development of Gestalt therapy over the coming half century (which would become the new age of relational psychology; Wheeler, 2011) owed more to Paul Goodman's (and Laura Perls's) legacy and concerns than to those of Fritz Perls, while still drawing and building on Fritz Perls's original fertile insight that in Gestalt psychology theory lay the potential for a radically new approach to psychotherapy based on the dynamism and authenticity of the individual's meaning making, relatively freed from the weight of old cultural assumptions and old therapeutic biases about adjustment and conformity. Without the original impetus of Perls's initiative and iconoclastic thinking, Goodman might never have considered the idea of self-development in relation to Gestalt psychology. Had Laura Perls not studied with Wertheimer and Gelb, Fritz Perls might never have intuited the fertile connections between his interests and the potential of Gestalt theory.

Continuing our story, it is to those next developments in Gestalt theory, based on and extending the methodology outlined by the founders, that we now turn.

THE ONGOING EVOLUTION OF THE GESTALT THERAPY MODEL AFTER GOODMAN AND PERLS

If Perls et al.'s presentation in *Gestalt Therapy: Excitement and growth in the human personality* in 1951 was revolutionary in its vision, it was also fairly sketchy when it came to method; it was short on tools and long on theory (including theoretical reflections on life, society, creativity, the arts, and what Goodman would term *anthropology*, by which he meant roughly the study of human nature and human behavior at a generalized, species-wide level). Nor did it directly address the issue of therapist training, other than by assuming the essential condition that therapists in training must have a deep experience of the process themselves as clients before working with others (a training requirement which is being dropped or minimized, disturbingly, by some schools of therapy today). By 1960 Fritz Perls had left New York for the West Coast, where he would spend the last decade of his life, soon leaving clinical practice altogether in favor of the public demonstration and workshop sessions at the Esalen Institute in California and elsewhere, for which both he and Gestalt therapy first became widely known (American Psychological Association, 2012; Perls, 1969). Paul Goodman also moved on from clinical work to a wider public role in the 1960s as a major writer and public spokesperson for progressive causes (Goodman, 1962; see also Stoehr, 1994a). Thus, it was up to Goodman's and Perls's associates and students to continue evolving the model in areas left open or undefined by the founders, or to deal with new issues and applications that arose in response to new research and new social challenges and new insights and opportunities in psychotherapy as a whole and psychology as a wider field.

THE WORK OF THE NEW YORK SCHOOL OF GESTALT THERAPY

After the publication of *Gestalt Therapy, Excitement and Growth in the Human Personality* in 1951 (F. Perls et al.), the original study group out of which the model had emerged soon gave rise to the New York Institute for Gestalt Therapy, long under the leadership of Laura Perls until shortly before her death in 1990. Laura Perls and Isadore From (Wysong & Rosenfeld, 1982), together with other senior associates, trained two generations of Gestalt therapists from across North America, Europe, and beyond, many of whom went on to write, teach, and found institutes of their own. Laura Perls wrote little over her long career (L. Perls, 1992), and From declined to write altogether; thus, their influence on the field was exerted mainly through their many students, some of whose work we discuss later.

Laura Perls was known for her focus on embodiment and move-ment and on the development of embodied self-supports (e.g., breathing, "grounding" in the sense of stance), whereas From placed great empha-sis on adhering closely to the founding text written in 1951, with a close focus on the typology of the resistances outlined earlier; in this sense From interpreted Gestalt as a "therapy of the ego" (his phrase; I. From, personal communication, October 11, 1992), referencing Goodman's definition of the ego function as the choosing and identifying function of the self (Perls et al., 1951, p. 429ff). Thus, it was left to the next generation to continue evolving the articulation of the basic relational process model of Gestalt therapy (Feder & Ronall, 1980) derived from Lewin's work in extending Gestalt psychology into a relational field model and also from the basic terms and emphases of Goodman's relational premises and concerns (Goodman, 1951; Stoehr, 1994a; see also his extensive body of work as a poet: Goodman, 1951), much of it on these same relational themes. Important and representative later writers of the New York school

include Lichtenberg (1990) on the application of Gestalt to social questions of prejudice and political oppression; Feder and Ronall (1980) on
group work; Frank (2001) on embodiment and relational development in
Gestalt perspective; and Bloom (2009) on relational, aesthetic, and ethical
considerations in clinical Gestalt perspective, to name just a few.

THE WORK OF THE GESTALT INSTITUTE OF CLEVELAND: THE CONTACT CYCLE MODEL

For the next steps in the evolution of the Gestalt model we turn to the
work of the teachers and writers of the Gestalt Institute of Cleveland (GIC),
who were trained directly by Fritz and Laura Perls, Paul Goodman, and
others of the founding New York group. Like Goodman, a number of the
founders of the GIC were educators and activists as well as clinicians, with
a core group coming out of social and organizational psychology at the
Case Western Institute in Cleveland. Several were also faculty members of
National Training Labs, which had been founded by Lewin in the late 1940s
to study group dynamics (E. Nevis, personal communication, July 18, 1976;
see also Polster & Polster, 1974, 1999). Thus, from the beginning, the founding GIC group carried the influence of Lewin's Gestalt-based work with
groups and organizations, as well as the clinical model and methodology
laid out by Goodman and Perls (Perls et al., 1951; Wheeler, 1991).

From the beginning, the teachers at GIC struggled with two related
training issues. First was how to make a Gestalt teaching curriculum that
would reach and be of introductory value to both clinical and nonclinical
audiences (including ever-growing numbers of students coming out of
the nascent movements of human potential and personal growth, who
might be from any walk of life and were studying Gestalt not necessarily
for professional reasons but in search of a more vivid aliveness, greater
satisfaction, and intensity of experience amid the routinization of modern life). Second was how to apply the concepts of Gestalt therapy to
larger social units than just the therapist–client dyad: couples, families,
groups, organizations, and society. All of these students and needs would
be well-served, these teachers felt, by a summary Gestalt model of how the
human system of experience and behavior works that could be taught to

and experienced by groups at different levels with different kinds of settings and goals. Such a model should be hands-on and portable yet not reductive and without losing the transformative enlivening spark of being desire-based and also experience-near that was key to the whole Gestalt therapy enterprise.

Their answer to both these needs lay in the creation of what has become known and widely used as the *cycle of experience* or *contact cycle model*, a schematic that could unfold richly into dimensions and implications for therapeutic, dyadic, organizational, or even culture-wide issues and skills. In essence, the model followed closely Perls and Goodman's outline of a contact sequence or stages of contact arc: pre- or forecontact, contacting and full or final contact, followed by post-contact (Goodman, 1951, p. 403). But the cycle model offered a much more detailed map of how therapy might be approached on the basis of this sequence and offered a key to relating the typology of resistances to contact to the particular stages of contact where they would arise, together with typical exercises and experiments for each resistance and each stage of the cycle (Polster & Polster, 1974). In addition, the cycle model served to organize a curriculum and method for training therapists and process facilitators as well as others. From the beginning, Gestalt has never made a rigid distinction—at least for initial training—between personal growth and development (the expansion and increasing complexity of contact capacities) and basic preparation or pretraining, at least for counseling and therapy. Here, of course, Gestalt is not different from the other "depth" methods; capacity and skills as a counselor or therapist have to rest on an extensive knowledge of one's issues, blind spots, and "growth edges," or in Gestalt terms, contact capacities and contact restrictions. By now the contact cycle has been presented in countless published works over the past half century, often with slight differences of organization or purpose from one presentation to another. Figure 3.1 shows one way of representing the cycle, as a self-contained circle (it has also often been an ongoing wave).

What are the uses and limitations of this cycle model, viewed now after some 50 years of varied use in a wide range of applications? We know that the map is not the territory (Korzybski, 1994), an idea that follows and restates Lewin's fertile work on perception, behavior, and field mapping of

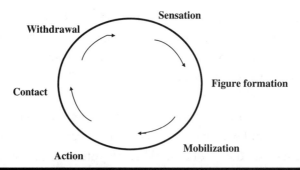

Figure 3.1

The cycle of experience model. From *Body Process: A Gestalt Approach to Working With the Body in Psychotherapy* (p. 91), by J. I. Kepner, 1987, Dalton, OH: Gardner Press. Copyright 1987 by Gardner Press. Adapted with permission.

the previous decade. Thus, the question is not whether the cycle model is a complete or final description of the contact process as Gestalt describes it; rather, the issue involves James's pragmatic question: Does this particular model (whether Gestalt therapy as a whole, or the cycle model specifically) capture something essential and render it useful to us in a way that can be usefully applied?

This pragmatic truth question becomes all the more relevant in schematic diagrams such as the cycle model; with schematics it is even more important to consider what is left out as well as what is captured usefully. The contact cycle as presented here (and as currently in wide use around the world in settings ranging from clinical to organizational) offers some clear strengths and user-friendly features: It is simple, teacher- and student-accessible, and lends itself easily to application at different levels of system—that is, individuals, couples and families, groups and organizations, and even cross-cultural study. Anglo-American culture, for example, is known, at least stereotypically, for moving quickly to the action stage of the cycle, with less attention spent, compared with some other cultures, in earlier, less action-oriented parts of the contact arc. Modern consumerist society has frequently been criticized as exaggerating the early sensation or desire phases of the cycle, while neglecting full awareness, full contact, and withdrawal, integration, and learning. When dealing with today's multicultural organizations and teams, as well as clinical issues across cultural boundaries, this kind of difference in cultural contact style or cultural signature becomes important to address; the cycle model offers a naturalistic and relatively value-neutral way of doing that.

In the same way, the contact cycle can also serve to highlight personal stylistic clashes or misfits across levels of system—for instance, the good or ill fit of one manager with the overall style and pace of the wider organization (or the nature of the problems at hand) or between members of the same systemic or relational level, such when one member of a couple typically delays decisions whereas the other tends to rush them (they often tend to polarize further from there, exaggerating the difference as each reacts to or tries to compensate for the extreme of the other).

At the same time, the cycle model suffers, as schematic models especially tend to, from its own strong points. By extracting the contact process from its context of a meaningful, actively relational social and experiential field, the cycle can seem to imply that contact is just a matter of an individual's internal impulse in isolation (e.g., hunger, pain or pleasure, sexual drive—even though Gestalt insists that even these seemingly biological needs and impulses are always shaped and conditioned with social meanings). Thus, quality of contact might seem to rest on just the uninterrupted flow of impulse energy toward tension release, no matter the context (a kind of throwback to a more primitive Freudian drive and tension-reduction model) rather than resting on the richness, complexity, relationality, and depth of meaning of the whole situational field and the whole gestalt being achieved, in dynamic integration with the complexly prefigured ground of previous contact and learning. (See Wheeler, 1991, for further discussion of the cycle model, pointing out its tendency to become "figure bound" by seeming to privilege the expression of desire or impulse without equal respect for the complexities, trade-offs, strategies, risks and stakes, and meanings that actually go into each moment of contact.) This oversimplification loses much of the richness of Lewin's (admittedly sloganistic) observation, "The need structures the *field*" (emphasis added; Marrow, 1969, p. 198), which underlined more clearly the holistic, figure–ground integration going on at all times, even in the simplest-seeming impulse satisfaction process. The point is that the cycle model is a useful tool for studying contact patterns as long as we remember that it is not a depiction of some ideal of contact.

The simple fact of arranging the elements of Goodman and Perls's stages of contact or contact sequences model into an ideal circle also tends to obscure what Goodman saw as a particular gift of the Gestalt model: the way the model emphasized the full contact stage, with its quality of timelessness or self-transcendence, that sense of losing oneself fully in an activity or a relational process (e.g., a lover and beloved or an artist absorbed in her media or that healthy melting of boundaries of time, space, and self that is creativity). This full or middle mode contact was an ideal of health and healthy creative process to Goodman, the payoff of working on the interruptions to contact the therapy was designed to attend to and repair.

The cycle model lends itself to a nonrelational interpretation of contact and of Gestalt theory more broadly. Indeed, Goodman and especially Fritz Perls at times seemed to imply that the model was most concerned with a healthy individual process, apart from the richness of the relational context that is always preconditioning our individuality as it emerges from the relational field.

Yet the Gestalt paradigm, from theory, research, and therapeutic applications alike, is inherently an *interactionist field model*, in which the integration of a unique individual perspective into and with a richly relational context, as depicted by Lewin, is the essence of human experience and the source of human behavior. The central concept of the Gestalt therapy model is *contact*, the process of resolving an experiential field into meaningful relationships among parts and parts, self and others, and self with ever-larger wholes of meaning. In this model the self and others are always the most significant parts and wholes of our experiential worlds, both individuals as whole selves and individuals as emergent dynamic parts of important groups of reference and belonging.

Finally, the cycle model can seem to reduce the Gestalt perspective to a transactional model, one in which contact, rather than being understood as the full ongoing, essential human process of meaning making that defines our species and informs our lives, is reduced to the everyday sense of the word *contact* as simply moving toward and then reaching or failing to reach the object of the motion. Gestalt therapy is not a model of object relations at all in the classic Freudian way of understanding behavior in terms of drives, defenses (against drive energy), and other people as objects of those drives. Rather, Gestalt is a relational field model of subject relations, in which full contact is the integral, meaning-making arc of understanding the self, the other person, and the field in an ever-evolving, ever-complexifying way. This perspective on contact—to which the authors of the cycle model itself would likely subscribe—can be lost in the acontextual simplification of the cycle model.

Thus, as the "me generations" of the 1970s and 1980s passed and a new decade (and new information technologies) brought forth a new age of complexity (Wheeler, 2008), the deep Lewinian and Gestalt psychology roots of Gestalt therapy have come increasingly to the fore as contemporary concerns shift from those of the too-repressed individual seeking self-expression to those of a whole-field, whole-world community struggling to find new and sustainable forms for dealing with each other in our ever-shrinking, ever-complexifying world. For Gestalt, the emergent outcome of these urgent concerns is a more fully and radically relational, fully and radically field-based contemporary practice.

THE RELATIONAL FIELD MODEL: CONTEMPORARY GESTALT PRACTICE

By stepping fully into our Lewinian, relational field roots and sources, contemporary Gestalt achieves further steps in the evolutionary theory process begun by Wertheimer and his associates a century ago, advanced and applied to real-life situations by Lewin and his followers, crystallized into a psychotherapy form by Goodman and the Perlses, and developed further over the past decades by a wide range of creative teachers and authors. We can trace this growing relational emphasis clearly through the work of Gestalt authors over the past several decades, including prominently (among many others) Polster and Polster (1974), emphasizing the relational nature of the resistances; Zinker (1978) on creativity and also working with couples; Nevis (1987), opening up the field of Gestalt work with organizations and large groups; Melnick and Nevis (1994) on dyadic process, the intimate couple, and the family; Kepner (1987, 1996) on relational embodiment and on trauma and healing; Wheeler (1991, 1996, 2000, 2003) on self-theory, development, shame and support, the human potential curriculum, and the application of Gestalt to systems constellations work; Yontef (1993) on dialogue and the I–thou relationship in therapy; Parlett (1992; in press) on field theory and on Gestalt as a curriculum for world citizenship; Lee (1996; 2004) on couples, shame, and ethics; Clemmens (2005) on addiction and on embodiment; McConville (1995) on adolescence and development; Jacobs and Hycner (2009) on relationship, dialogue, and intersubjectivity; Roberts (1999) on field theory and creativity; Ullman (2005) on Lewin's work and on spirituality in Gestalt; Spagnuolo Lobb (2013) on empathy and relationship; Bloom (2009) on relationship, aesthetics, and ethics; and many more (to name just a few of the writers in the English language who have emphasized and developed the relational field perspective). This relational evolution in our understanding and expression of the Gestalt therapy model, strongly informed and validated by the emergent neuroscience revolution as well as by clinical experience, has a number of direct dimensions and implications that together make up contemporary Gestalt.

Self-Theory and the Understanding of the Individual Self

Humans are the most distinctly, uniquely individual of all animals and also the most complexly socially embedded species found in nature. This inherent duality of human nature and process—complex social embeddedness and complex individual creativity—is at the heart of our more complex Gestalt understanding of how we organize and construct our social field of experience in unique interpretive ways and also how we are (pre)organized by that same field, not just in early development but also in dynamic interaction all through life. This is the essence of Gestalt's answer to James's challenge of a century ago—how we ever manage to organize the potential sensory overload of our infinitely variable social field. Following Lewin's model, we map a field (especially a social field) in relation to the patterns we are predisposed (preconditioned) by our nature and by past social experience to attend to (or impose inflexibly) in relation to our perception of the needs, emotional states, intentions, goals, and values that reflect our unique creative interpretive synthesis of our present self-state (Wheeler, 2000, 2011). (For influential source discussions of these and related ideas from parallel traditions that have interacted deeply with Gestalt psychology, see Gergen, 2011, for a social constructionist account of how this works on a cultural level; Schore, 2009, and Siegel, 2012, for a contemporary interpersonal neurobiology discussion of how this brain plasticity continues to operate throughout our lives; and Stolorow, Atwood, & Orange, 2002, for an intersubjective and psychoanalytic discussion of these dynamics in the therapy session.)

Key to this contemporary relational field Gestalt understanding is the new knowledge coming from contemporary evolutionary biology (Hrdy, 2009; D. S. Wilson, 2007). We understand more today—and will continue to deepen this understanding as research continues to unfold and expand in this area—about the prematurity of our prefrontal cortex (PFC) at birth, that newest part of our evolved brain that sets us apart from our closest animal relations. The fact that our PFC is not wired at birth is key to what enables our open-ended creativity (because we are so extensively freed from the rigidity of inborn instinct patterns; see D. S. Wilson, 2007). Early relational and cultural patterning then takes the place of fixed instincts, giving us enough patterning to cope with complex social variability. This helps us understand the extremely deep influence of culture, which can have almost the force of biological instinct, and also shows us the source of most of the issues and problems our clients bring to us: too rigid or otherwise dysfunctional areas of early patterning, which is what happens when our nervous system is forced to adapt to overwhelming stress or trauma with insufficient relational support, the context of what we call today *developmental trauma*, or trauma patterns arising more from neglect than from assault (though sadly, both can and do often occur together; see Axelsson, in press). The outcome, as we see continually in our practices, is a rigid (or rigidly disorganized) self-process in which complex integrative PFC activation is not available to the person, who remains stuck in a repetitive, unsatisfying cycle of avoidance or other dysfunction in some areas of life until a more healthy, natural gestalt process of ongoing and ever-more complex creative response can be supported and restored.

This is how Gestalt therapy relational self-theory aims to do full justice to both these poles of our integral being: the uniquely individual and the radically social. This means that we view the individual as uniquely emergent from a dynamic social field of relationships (thus the term *relational field Gestalt;* see Wheeler, 2000, 2011). Each of us sees and expresses a unique viewpoint in and from a constantly interactive web of dynamic social influence, energy, and belonging (Wheeler, 2011). Each of us has the capacity, with support, to express and evolve our self-process and our relational social nature as part of larger wholes of being and meaning in unique and ever-more complex, creative forms.

These views contrast fundamentally with an older self-paradigm in Western culture. Earlier versions of a classic Freudian model, classic behaviorism, and indeed the individualist self-ideal in Western culture generally, have considered the individual and her or his development first and the relationship as something that is secondary to this primary reality (*secondary process* in Freud; see Wheeler, 2000). Relational field Gestalt completely reverses this (in parallel with the contemporary evolution of the other major models). This way of understanding human nature—who we are in the most basic sense—is more complex than that older paradigm, with consequences for our understanding of development, clinical issues, shame and support, and change, as outlined next.

The Developmental Model and the Definition of Health

Perls viewed healthy maturity, the ideal of growth and maturation, as the progress from other-supports to self-supports (see Perls, 1969). As a slogan, this was useful and had appeal as a description of a healthy critical process in that oppressively conformist cultural and historical context (the mass fascistic times of the early and mid-20th century), but such a formulation of the goals of development and health fails to take account of the full relational legacy of Gestalt psychology, particularly as formulated by Lewin. Today, we expand on that picture further by reaching deeper into the full Gestalt theory background of human process to support the following definitions.

Development

In relational Gestalt perspective, *growth* is the coconstruction of an increasingly complex integrated resolution of relational experience and capacity. In childhood development this means incorporating the increasing potential capacities of the growing child into wider and wider spheres of relationship, action, and meaning as the child's developmental abilities mature and take the child into wider and wider spheres of action and learning. The relational field Gestalt model defines *development* as the ongoing coconstruction of wider and more complex wholes of meaning and action that serve to enable the person to continue growing, creating, and resolving ever-more complex understanding, which serves in turn as a platform for ever-more creative and complex actions and experiences. This view of development is lifelong and open-ended, based on relationships, creativity, and the crucial capacity to tolerate and meaningfully resolve complexity and ambiguity in ever-more complex settings and situations over the life span. Growth, in the Gestalt view, never stops. This leads to a different—in a sense, double—view of health and the goals of therapy.

The Goals of Therapy and the Definition of Health

The goal of Gestalt therapy is a complex, doubly dimensioned one. *Health*, in this relational field creative and evolutionary view of self and self-process, is the capacity to cocreate new patterns of experience, action, and understanding that serve to support further evolution of ever-increased complexity of relationship and understanding. This means, among other things, that Gestalt is particularly well-suited for supporting work with an older demographic as well as other age groups: Although physical abilities eventually decline with age, we know today that the human brain's capacity to continue to create and elaborate increasingly complex wholes of meaning and understanding—barring organic illness—only deepens with age. The cocreation of meaning is what the Gestalt model—and Gestalt definitions of health and development—are all about.

Relationship and Presence: Showing Up

Therapists have long known that the capacity to "show up" and be in an attuned, empathic relationship with our client is absolutely key to therapeutic progress and outcome (see much more about this crucial predictor in therapeutic outcomes in Chapter 5). Today, standing as we do at the richly fermenting beginnings of the neuropsychology revolution that is transforming our field, we are beginning to know much more about what showing up in a relationship really means and why that capacity in the therapist is so crucial and effective. We examine this more deeply in Chapter 6; meanwhile, it is important to note that the arc of developmental capacity and the definition of health here are dependent on—and synonymous with—an increase in integral response capacity in the brain (the simultaneous activation of multiple brain centers in response to self, situations, and other people; e.g., empathic, embodied, emotive, facial, autobiographical, and other brain centers; see Siegel, 2010, 2012). In neurobiological terms, this is the increasing capacity for complexity discussed earlier (see A. N. Schore, 2009; J. R. Schore & Schore, 2008).

From its beginnings, Gestalt has been directly focused on pattern formation and pattern recognition, the remarkably developed human capacity to perceive a variable environment by selecting and attending to patterns (detailed in Chapter 2) and forming and modifying behavior patterns or sequences so as to automate or habituate complex behavioral repertoires. This pattern creation (i.e., learning) is our essential strategy to free up attentional space for the most urgent new condition in the present situation (the key to our human creative capacity to manage a near-infinite range of variability, especially social variability). These created behavioral strings or patterned sequences are our functional adaptation to managing background, or the familiar aspects of a situation, while leaving us free to attend to the most urgent need or most challenging new feature of that situation. This works well in humans—most of the time. When this natural gestalt-forming process breaks down, with rigid, out-of-date response patterns being transferred—mostly involuntarily—to new situations, it produces the dysfunctional, unsatisfying results—which may often be mystifying to the clients themselves—that bring our clients into therapy.

Those "stuck" learned patterns of experience, behavior, and meaning are what therapy is all about. A gift of this perspective is helping us to better understand how and why therapist presence makes such a difference: When the therapist shows up in this full, integrated way (Siegel, 2012), a pattern of multiple-center activation occurs in the client's brain. This means the client has more integrative or creative PFC capacity in the therapist's attuned presence than he or she likely will in other challenging situations that provoke or evoke those same old, nonproductive responses (much like what earlier models called *defenses*, or the original Gestalt therapy model called *resistance* or *interruptions to contact;* see the earlier discussion).

This further clarifies Goodman's paradoxical image of therapy as a safe emergency. The situation is an emergency in the sense that it is evoking or provoking overlearned, probably anxiety-based, no longer functional response patterns, including emotions, understanding and predictions, and behavioral responses (i.e., a familiar stuck defense). Still, the emergency, although real (because the relationship is real), is relatively safe because the stakes are lower (than out there in the world of heavier consequences for "wrong" responses) and because of the additional support of the therapist's full presence, in the ways outlined previously.

Thus, in relational field Gestalt we emphasize that therapist presence and the therapist–client relationship are not preconditions or a pretherapy stage; they are our first, most impactful, and most ongoing active interventions all through the therapy. In Gestalt therapy the coconstruction of the relationship is the therapy as well as the lab in which the most experiments can be made (explicitly or organically, as the therapist facilitates the measured challenge for greater and greater capacity for relational complexity in the growing client).

Support and Shame

Another strength of Gestalt is a new and deeper understanding of what we mean by *support* in a relational field model—and with this new understanding we gain a new capacity to deal directly and creatively with that most pervasively challenging of therapeutic issues and topics: shame. If we take a Lewinian relational field model seriously, we can say (tautologically but meaningfully) that whatever happens in a field is supported and enabled by the conditions of that field. Thus, at any moment, *support* means all the conditions that promote, support, and favor what is happening. In a relational field model, one's inner world is not something separated from one's field of experience; rather, the relative distinctions *inner* and *outer* experience simply refer to a different kind of attentional focus and different ways of registering "what's happening" subjectively. Thus, experiences and memories such as hope, willpower, confidence in one's abilities, past experience overcoming and achieving in some relevant area—all those kinds of resources that we think of as inner—are also field conditions that condition behavior and experience.

These inner field conditions interact dynamically with external field conditions such as perceived opportunities and obstacles and, above all, the expected perceptions of support or lack of support from other people, particularly other people perceived as powerful or personally important. Thus, *field conditions* are the whole experiential field, one's inner world and outer world (which, most important, includes oneself and other significant people). Note how this also includes one's perception, attribution, and imagination of others' inner experience and motivations and thus their likely next behavior. One has to know these areas of the field; they comprise an essential part of the best available interpretation of the conditions of the situation. Too rigid patterns of assumptions about others on the basis of trauma or lack of support in the past are a huge impediment to ongoing growth and healthy, satisfying responses and relationships in present life. Learning how to manage and hold those assumptions more lightly and how to consider other interpretations of the field, plus learning new skills for dialogue and inquiry, will all be a correspondingly large part of therapy (see Wheeler, 1996, 2000). This is a much broader, richer, and we argue, more useful understanding of support as the dynamic conditioning factors of one's experience and behavior. Armed with this understanding, one can then take a more productive approach to that universally problematic human challenge: the issue of shame.

Shame, from a relational field perspective, is first and always a crucial aspect of pervasive social embeddedness, the way our individuality emerges from a holistic social and relational web of shared interactive being. For humans—most acutely in our long, helpless childhood and then throughout life—the capacity to attune to, read, anticipate, and manage the reactions of others is key to our surviving and thriving. Shame is the sense that this necessary web of coparticipatory human existence is thinning, rupturing or being threatened with rupture, or pulling away from the individual (leaving him or her more alone). Seen in this way, shame is an essential part of our affective tool kit, sensitizing us to the social reactions or lack of support around us so that we can make necessary adjustments and possibly fall in line with the social norm—or, equally possibly, organize more support to make a change in the direction of more choice and creativity in what is acceptable in that social field. A third alternative is to take the shame signal to leave that social field and find a new one (for further discussion, see Lee, 1996; Wheeler, 1996, 1997).

This sensitivity to the social field does not have to be a paralyzing experience—it merely depends on past experiences of support or social rupture. In the regular, healthy flow of the interactive relational process, an early sign of shame (others not meeting or supporting one's presence or action) can be simply a social signal to "step up" other supports (i.e., inner supports and also the mobilization of memory of supports from others perhaps not present) so that the sum of supportive conditions in the present field is great enough to permit one to operate creatively, freely, and with a low enough sense of risks and stakes that one still has the capacity to generate more complex, productive behaviors (i.e., new ways of encountering new or old challenges). In practice, this can be as familiar and simple as trying harder, enlisting others in support, attending more to others' discomfort, reaching for practiced self-support skills (e.g., breathing, thought stopping or interrupting, becoming reinspired through evoking other relationships and larger meanings).

This is the case for the healthy, supported individual for whom past experience has been affirming enough to provide flexibility to continue responding creatively, even under challenge. However, evocations and repetitions of experiences occur when the lack of affirmation from others creates a more desperate emergency (and perhaps a physically dangerous, abusive, or panicking loss of safety and support, especially in childhood). If *trauma* involves a situation that overwhelms the nervous system's capacity to respond in an integrated way, a *trauma disorder* is persistent reactivity (at least to certain situations or stimuli) as a habit pattern in the nervous system so deeply imprinted that it bypasses the PFC, with reactions governed by the faster, more primitive response centers (the familiar and paralyzing fight–flight–freeze reaction). Significantly, it is only in trauma patterns that we find the one-to-one, stimulus–response patterns unmediated by PFC, meaning making, and strategic and decisional processes that were the paradigm for understanding human behavior a century ago in the pre-Gestalt associationist model discussed in Chapter 2.

Thus, in this sense, shame—the loss of a field of social resonance and support—is always a central dynamic in trauma and a central issue in trauma healing and recovery. In an older pre-Gestalt individualist self-model, shame was understood more simplistically as a sense of inferiority (which should be overcome with maturity, a social "should" that only leads to a vicious circle of shame about shame, hiding the shame feelings, and further isolation; see Wheeler, 1996). Our approach to working with shame dynamics is to first revalorize and validate shame as a part of our inherent social capacities for navigating complex social fields, sensing where relational support is weak or missing and helping to strategize and respond creatively. Second, shame feelings are met with greater empathic attunement (combined with great respect for boundaries and not invading or correcting the client at vulnerable moments). This helps us understand, for instance, why it can be reshaming to try to talk people out of their shame feelings (e.g., "You shouldn't feel that way"; such words are meant well but probably also express the therapist's discomfort with feelings of shame; for more discussion of this key dynamic in therapy and in development and life, see Wheeler, 1996).

A Relational Field Gestalt Theory of Change

The evolution of the contemporary relational field Gestalt model to include the full relational implications of the Lewinian model underlying Goodman and the Perlses' work opens up our understanding of a relational field Gestalt theory or model of change. If experience and the behavior that emerges from our integrated experiential field are always outcomes of field conditions of support, it follows that any significant change in behavior (and experience) depends on a change in those field conditions of support. This may seem like a circular proposition or tautology, but in practice we believe this exploration of new supports to be one of the most often neglected areas in the therapy process and one of the most important, directly useable contributions of the Gestalt perspective (equally applicable under any model). Therapy, after all, is about change, hopefully and most often change desired and codesigned by and with the client in line with her or his goals and values. In addition to exploring *ground* (the dynamic issues or fears holding a given nonfunctional pattern in place and getting in the way of needed change), and along with experimenting with new desired behaviors both within and outside the therapy session, the crucial additional step for change to be lasting is to identify and activate new, additional supports in the experiential field that will promote the new desired behavior (and often interrupt or lessen support for the old, undesired, and fixed or repetitive pattern).

These new supports can come from the inner and/or outer experiential field, and in most instances will be most effective if they come from both arenas. In practice, this idea of identifying social or "other" supports may often seem startling or unnatural (or downright weak) at first to the client; in our individualistic culture we are habitually supported and expected to think only of self-supports when we are designing (and supporting) intentions for change. Because we are often dealing with behaviors and areas the client has tried many times and ways of changing before without success, these self-supports are often strongly tinged with shame (e.g., "If I would just try harder," "The problem is my weak willpower," or other such self-deprecating responses).

There is nothing wrong with trying harder; indeed, that is probably the way we achieve most of our intentional changes. However, people do not tend to come to counseling with issues for which trying harder alone has been successful; rather, the things people want counseling for (we know this well from repetitive and unfulfilling relational patterns and aspects in some parts of our lives) are likely to be issues that are strongly dynamically charged with anxiety, fear, and shame. This is where adding outer or "other" supports can be revelatory and can unblock issues that may have been stuck for many years (for more discussion of this issue in practice, see the case of the couple, among others, in Chapter 4).

Restating this field-relational Gestalt theory of change now, we can say: for any change in behavior and experience to occur and last (your own behavior or your client's), there must be some change in the dynamic pattern of supports in the whole field. Conversely, a significant change in the pattern of supports in the experiential field ("positive" and "negative" supports alike) will produce a change in behavior and experience in your client's life, or in your own. Taken together, these thematic theory points represent and summarize key aspects of the ongoing evolution of Gestalt therapy theory, bringing the contemporary articulation of theory and method more fully in line with those basic Gestalt psychology insights discussed in Chapter 2, which have proved so pervasive and durable across a century of research and incorporation into other models.

WIDER IMPACT

Looking back over the half century since Goodman and Perls cocreated their seminal volume presenting their revolutionary approach, what can we say about the impact of Gestalt therapy on the wider field? First, it would be difficult to overstate the impact, which was at first quite slow and then gathered steam at the end of the 1950s, of the introduction of the Gestalt model (and other present-centered approaches) on the world of psychotherapy and on the evolution of nearly all major models of psychotherapy since that time. Much like the impact of Gestalt psychology on the wider field of psychology, there are few major models of psychotherapy today that have not adopted some of the chief hallmarks of the then-radical Goodman–Perls model: (a) the here-and-now, present-life-situation focus; (b) the focus on developmental challenge and response in place of an older emphasis on pathology and cure; (c) the emphasis on affect, emotion, and body experience; (d) the cultivation of an authentic encounter and real (if still bounded) relationship between therapist and client; (e) the use of the therapy situation as a here-and-now experimental relational lab; (f) a radical respect for and focus on the client's agency and validity as a coconstructer of her or his values, meanings, and criteria for making choices organizing his or her life, together often with (g) a more nuanced, judicious use of the therapist's experience as a rich source of information for the client to know and integrate in her or his navigation of relationship and growth of relational capacity. Many other aspects and dimensions of the model, such as the fuller use of embodied experience and data, the strong emphasis on self-expression and creativity, the radical revisioning of the therapist's role as a full coparticipant or observer in the process, and the revalorization of desire and passion, remain more specifically characteristic of Gestalt therapy, in contrast to some other contemporary models.

The model was revolutionary, and as such it contributed to and became part of an even wider revolution in psychotherapy over the coming decades as therapy shifted from an elite to a mass phenomenon and widened extensively from a focus on pathology and dysfunction to a new interest in the depth and quality of satisfaction of each person's life journey in our overwhelmingly complex, often deeply undersupported contemporary lives. For all its remarkable contributions and influence and with all its radical emphasis on relationship and positive constructive capacities (both such strong therapy themes today), particular key elements needed today for a fully realized, fully relational field-based contemporary Gestalt therapy theory and methodology were still un- or underdeveloped in the Goodman–Perls model. They include a fully intersubjective model of self and relationship, a fully relational model of attachment and development, an articulated model of working with shame and support, a neurologically coherent understanding of trauma and recovery, and (integrating all of these) a fully relational field Gestalt theory of change. Having reviewed these further developments and outlined the hallmarks of a contemporary, field-theory-based relational Gestalt therapy, we turn in Chapter 4 to the application of the model with a diverse range of clients, types of cases, and settings. Gestalt therapy is about the enactment of actual living: fuller presence in ourselves and our worlds, richer and deeper relational capacity, greater capacity for passion and satisfaction in living, and a deeper sense of meaning making in our lives.

4

The Therapeutic Process

In this chapter, we illustrate, apply, and in the process, further develop the concepts introduced earlier in this book. Case studies give life to theory, and as we hope you have already realized from the earlier discussion, Gestalt is about finding and enlivening the themes and places in our lives and experience that are stuck, deadened, not satisfying our deepest yearnings for connection and meaning, and not supporting new growth in our capacity to support and use ever-more complex relational and experiential processes all through life. Thus, in this chapter we provide case accounts in a Gestalt way by giving you not just the facts but also our experience of the client and the exchange we experienced and made meaning of. Our hope is that you will be able to see through our eyes and think and feel through our minds and hearts as we worked as creatively as we could to be fully present with our clients and to be of service to them when their development was blocked or deadened, as well as at times when they were in desperate crisis.

http://dx.doi.org/10.1037/14527-004
Gestalt Therapy, by G. Wheeler and L. Axelsson

The cases discussed here are extracts and vignettes, not complete accounts. We have made every effort to protect each client's identity. We select the cases to illustrate particular dimensions, potentials, and applications of Gestalt methodology, with accent on where Gestalt might support a greater focus on some dynamic aspect or issue or intervention that is different from other approaches; we try to give only enough of the background (and of the rest of the story after the point illustrated) for readers to get the feel of the situation and be oriented to the points we want to highlight. Different aspects of Gestalt theory and method will come to the fore in different cases, and we have tried to select, in this brief format, a broad range of types of clients (adults and children, couples, and clients with diverse cultural identities, sexual identities, ages, and parent and nonparent status, among other differences). We invite you to note again that we, the coauthors, belong to different generations and different genders, we hail from different national and cultural origins, and we have quite different professional histories (with significant overlap: Both of us have worked with children and adults in public mental health and private practice settings and in schools and organizations as both counselors and consultants as well as coaches). This is the human variation that is always present, though it may be more or less attended to in various methods. Gestalt is founded on these dynamics of diversity, with its long, research-based dual legacy of individual uniqueness (the constructivist perspective we wrote about in Chapter 2, that founding contribution of Gestalt and Gestalt research that revolutionized all of psychology) plus Gestalt theory's emphasis on coconstructionism, our inherent, always-present embeddedness in our relational context and dynamic, past, present, and anticipated future.

How do we find our way in all this rich complexity without reducing or simplifying away the dynamics that make up the present field conditions of each emergent consciousness in each interaction? A particular Gestalt move that occurs repeatedly in the vignettes is the emphasis on our "showing up" with full and embodied emotional attunement to other and to self. This self and other awareness is a hallmark of Gestalt and offers us a kind of touchstone for understanding the here-and-now field conditions (by "checking in" with one's own body and emotions) and then either mentioning them explicitly or using them as a guide to our inquiry or other experiments with the client, depending on our assessment of his or her capacity for using that kind of direct, person-to-person contact (that essential self and social skill that will certainly be a developmental goal and benchmark for the client's evolving capacities throughout our work). Self and other awareness also helps us in attuning to the client and looking for how that attunement may be turned into relational contact in a way the client can use, relax into, and grow from.

This special attention follows from our discussion in the previous chapters of the importance of attuned, empathic relational contact as the key precondition for beginning to relax old, rigid patterns of engagement and self and other organization that were established behaviorally and neurologically often long ago under conditions of inadequate support, or worse. As we seek this "sweet zone" of attuned engagement (the zone for experiment, new experience, and new integration that is growth), we pay attention to neurological states of arousal or disorganization—our own as well as the client's—as we perceive and register the activation in our own state of arousal and awareness. In particular, this includes awareness and attunement to the nervous system (our own as well as the client's). This kind of attending is crucial, because as relational Gestalt therapists, we focus not just on offering support from us or support as a checklist of behaviors but also on the actual experience of support by the client her- or himself. As we watch for signs of dis-arousal and more coherent organization (e.g., Siegel, 2010) in the client, we begin to understand what is facilitative and what causes "flooding" for this client in this situation at this moment. When we can meet and attune to this (without being lost in it), we are in the zone of the kind of contact between us that serves the client, and the work unfolds from there.

One final note in a contemporary register in preparation for the discussions: Some of the most basic, structural ways we show support include concrete, seemingly simple actions such as not having a cell phone that is turned on and can disrupt us and an office space that provides privacy and can block outside distractions. We start the session on time, do not keep the client waiting, and try to demonstrate our attentiveness by facing her or him and maintaining an amount of eye contact that seems to be the most comfortable and useable for the client at that moment. The last of these points (the amount of eye contact) is one of our first experiments in the therapy (which we may or may not elect to share with the client at this early point—if eye contact is uncomfortable, it is not likely the time to comment on that fact yet). The other points may seem unnecessary to mention, but we live in a time when turning away and reading or even answering a text in the middle of a conversation is normative. The point is to signal to the client that this is not a time for multitasking (at least for the therapist) but a time and space to focus on the client's experience. This is something that may have been partially or wholly missing in the client's development (or worse—the attention was there and unsafe).

In true Gestalt fashion, we then look for an opportunity to inquire how that "experiment" of privileged personal focus is going, both so we can offer more attunement and accommodation and so the client has an opportunity to experience that crucial self-inquiry step that will be so useful in therapy and in life ("How is this feeling for me right now? What do I want? What do I need?") and feel him- or herself stepping into an active cocreative role in the process of the therapeutic encounter.

MARIE: PUZZLES AND MODULATION OF CONTACT

Thirteen-year-old Marie, a Caucasian girl living with her parents and two younger brothers in a small rural farming community, was brought to therapy by her parents. She suffered from severe social anxiety and some general anxiety as well. During our intake session she was able to express that she did not like talking and that her previous therapist had always asked her question after question. This only made her feel more anxious. I (LA) promised her that there were other ways we could work, ways that did not include me firing questions at her, which she would then have to try to answer. I thanked her for this clarity (especially because she "didn't like to talk"), which would serve us in building our relationship.

We started out playing board games, none of which looked "therapeutic" from the outside; this helped us get to know each other and negotiate together the issue of trust, at least on the level of building familiarity and managing expectations as we began to relate to one another. I let Marie pick the games, but even that was a difficult task, and often she would freeze in her anxiety and ask me to pick one. After a few sessions like this, I began picking out three games and asking her whether there was one game of these three she did not want to play. As I did this I also asked her to rate her anxiety and tell me if having to make this choice made her anxiety too high and unmanageable. These concrete, "here and now" questions seemed more manageable than the more probing kind she had warned me about. Marie reported that when I asked this, her anxiety did become higher but not unmanageable. When I asked whether she could then pick one of the two games left, the game she wanted to play, she reported that her anxiety became too intense. I thanked her for helping our process by telling me, and I picked one of the two games myself.

This was Gestalt contact work, slowed down to meet the client in her proximal learning zone of mild but moderate anxiety and at the same time providing Marie with a model and an experience of how power and closeness in relational exchange could be shared and modulated. Every time we were at the point of choosing the next game I would encourage her to check in with herself to see where her anxiety level was, and she would report back to me, usually on a scale of 1 to 10. From time to time I would ask whether she was ready to choose not just which of the three games to exclude but also which of the two games to play. Sometimes she was able to pick the game, and when that happened I would invite her to check in with herself to see whether she could tell what made her able to make the choice this time but not other times. I would also ask what she believed would happen if she chose which game to play. I did not expect an answer, and I did not need one; my intention was to help her increase her awareness. A few months into the therapy she told me that she was afraid to pick the wrong game, a game I did not want to play. I did not probe this answer further at the time; I just thanked her for this new awareness and sharing.

After a few more sessions I introduced art materials as one of the three activities. The first few times she picked that activity as the one she did not want to do, but later she began leaving it as one of the two for me to choose from. The times I picked the art materials I did not ask her to make something specific but allowed her to create whatever she came up with, just experimenting with mixing colors or some more figurative picture.

During this period, which lasted several months, I did not use many words; I mostly followed her lead of just hanging out together. If I did experiment with asking her a few questions about her anxiety outside the therapy room, she would withdraw and stop, reverting to giving me her default one-word answers, which told me I was pushing her over her anxiety threshold. One day she answered that she found it difficult when I looked at her while she did her art projects. I asked her whether she wanted me to turn my back to her, and she answered with a clear yes. During quite a few sessions she started asking me to turn my back to her while she drew or painted. I would always do this, letting her know in this direct, enacted way that I respected her boundaries and that she had the power to affect her environment in a way that helped her. I also asked her how my turning my back toward her made a difference in her body, again coming back to the immense resource her body could be for helping her track and modulate her anxiety.

I sometimes wrote a question on a piece of paper because it seemed easier for her to communicate in written form. At one point I suggested hanging a blanket over two chairs so there was a wall between us, to see whether that would make it even easier for her to be in the room with me, compared with having me turn my back to her. As we tried this, I continued with the written communication, writing a question then crumpling the paper into a ball and tossing it over the wall of the blanket. She would then write the answer and throw the paper back to me. The messages back and forth were about what she wanted to do in the sessions with me and how difficult it was for her to make these decisions. Slowly, at her pace, we were finding our own creative way toward a deeper, fuller exchange, expression, and trust.

After about half a year Marie had grown more comfortable with the choices she could make in the therapy room with me. At this point she was able to pick what she wanted to do for the session, sometimes with more anxiety than others, but no matter what the level of anxiety, our focus was on the experiential quality of the anxious state, where she felt it in her body, sometimes what she anticipated as a possible bad outcome, and the words she was telling herself as she tried to choose.

In one session she asked whether I had a puzzle, saying she really liked doing them. I told her I shared that interest and promised her I would bring some puzzles from home the following session. Realizing that doing a 1,000-piece puzzle is something that would take longer than one session, I also brought in a felt blanket and a roller to roll up and store the puzzle between sessions. At this point the ability to focus on the puzzle was enough of a regulator for Marie, a big step forward from when she preferred to have me turn my back to her or even sit on the other side of the blanket/wall only communicating through notes tossed back and forth. As her anxiety became lower she became increasingly verbal, even though she still sat quietly for a minute or two before she answered a question. Many a time although I expected she was not going to answer a question at all and just needed to be quiet, she all of a sudden gave me a long answer. My understanding was simply that she needed time to check in with her body, perhaps settle her anxiety, and make sure she could feel our connection strongly enough for her to share her thoughts with me.

Marie was starting high school, and as the beginning of school approached, her anticipatory anxiety increased sharply. As we sat on the floor putting together the pieces of the puzzle, we also put together the different pieces of her anxiety puzzle. She was slowly able to tell me how much she wanted to fit in with her peers but also that she did not want to give up who she was. She worried what others would think about her. When I suggested that part of the anxiety she still experienced in the therapy room with me might be that she worried what I might think about her, she was able to confirm this as true. My suggestion was that she check in with herself before sharing her thoughts and remind herself she always had the choice of either saying what she was thinking, deciding to say nothing at all, or stating the feeling of anxiety out loud. When she started to do this, she found that speaking about her anxiety often led her to be able to state what she thought had been hard to share. In this way we were experimenting with, without naming it, the essential skill of actively modulating the contact difficulty. That is, instead of the all-or-nothing choice of silence or intense, unmanageable anxiety, there is the "middle" choice: naming the difficult action and naming the feeling that is present.

As we were putting together the puzzle and talking about school before and after she started the fall semester, we often played around with the different parts she described having inside her head. One was just wanting to fit in, to be a regular teenager, whereas another part was wanting to be just who she was; in addition, she wanted to be who she was but with more attitude. Different parts gave her more or less anxiety in different situations, but as she became more aware of the choices she could make as to how to present herself, she reported feeling less anxious at school. I encouraged her to explore the new part, the one with the most attitude, to help her practice being more assertive, because that was the part that gave her the most anxiety.

While we were putting together the puzzle in one of the sessions (with me nonchalantly asking questions), I asked her what would happen if she did not have anxiety and how it would change her life, a question I had asked on a few occasions throughout our work together. This time she became quiet, and I asked her to check in about her anxiety level. She reported feeling very anxious, saying she was worried what I would think about her if she answered the question. I told her I doubted she was able to say anything that would make me like her less but that she needed to check in with herself if she was ready to take that risk. After a few minutes sitting quietly and working on the puzzle, she told me that without her anxiety she would receive less attention. This represented a breakthrough, a huge summing up of our work together. I felt celebratory. She was distancing herself from the experience of anxiety in a whole new way: Instead of identifying with it and being taken over by it, she was looking at it as a "part" in itself, a feeling or function that might serve a purpose or get in the way but that in any case she could step apart from and look at, with me, from some other deeper, more capable part of her developing sense of self. I did not convey any of this to Marie at the time. My response was to reflect what she had shared, remarking in the most normalizing way I could that I could see how that must make it quite difficult at times to leave the anxiety behind.

CARLOS: SUPPORT AT ANY PRICE

One wants to be loved, in lack thereof admired, in lack thereof feared, in lack
thereof loathed and despised. One wants to instill some sort of emotion in
people. The soul trembles before emptiness and desires contact at any price.

—Hjalmar Söderberg [Translated by Lena Axelsson]

A conceptual dilemma in discussing support from a Gestalt perspective is the notion of inner and outer support, if there is any distinction as to where support is coming from. After all, even when we are alone, the support we draw on is not something that comes from within but something that once was developed in relationship; we reference absent relationships, communities, and groups implicitly or explicitly. The same goes for when we perceive the support as coming from our surroundings: We can perceive and use it as support because at some earlier point in our lives we have been able to internalize the sense of belonging, in some way deserving and receiving support.

Gestalt theory supports shifting our way of looking at our world to a more relational view. We are cocreating our experiences, not just with the people who are currently present with us, but to a greater or lesser extent with every significant person and experience we have had up to that point in our lives (for better and, sadly, sometimes for worse). Support grows out of the contact we have and have had with our social and relational environment. As support grew in the past or grows now, it conditions our expectations about what is and is not going to be easy or even possible (or harder or even unthinkable) in current or upcoming relationships or situations.

We predict outcomes from previous experiences; we want to create patterns. An infant who cries and is picked up by a caregiver to be held and soothed will on a deep level see and come to expect the pattern of "distress/ express/get met with comfort and help" (Bowlby, 1994; A. N. Schore, 2003; Tronick, 2007). Whoever has a consistent experience of being with caregivers who meet them at their level of excitement or withdrawal will then begin to develop a regulated nervous system and the ability to self-soothe, growing out of the experience that there are people around who are there when they are needed. As the infant grows up, when there is a negative incident on the playground or at school (as there will inevitably be as we move out into wider life circles), for example, he or she will seek out support from an adult or possibly another child in the surroundings at the time or later when she or he gets home.

An infant who is not picked up when crying or who is not changed or fed on a regular basis within his or her window of tolerance when it comes to discomfort, an infant who has caregivers who are not available or able to attune to the infant's level of excitement or withdrawal, will establish and then experience a different, more reactive brain pattern and a less regulated nervous system. When this infant grows older he or she will not have the sense of having much support available in her or his world. Instead of running to the yard duty teacher or a friend at school (why would one do that if one did not see the point of reaching out for support?), this child might instead punch the child who may have accidentally bumped into him or her. Given the less regulated nervous system that, from a lower or less strategic region of the brain, makes this child more prone to act impulsively, we might have what many will see as a "problem child." For some of the clients we work with, the wish to feel supported and the deep-rooted longing to find a group or at least one or two individuals who the client believe supports them can lead to situations of risk and danger, in the extreme even a matter of life and death.

This was the case with Carlos, who came to me (LA) as a seventh grader toward the end of the school year, already on the local police list for his known involvement with gangs. He was in foster care, with a mother who was a drug addict and a father whose whereabouts were unknown and who was addicted to marijuana and alcohol to some degree. Carlos had a report card with a straight line of Fs. It was not love at first sight between Carlos and me. On the contrary, he was brought in by his social worker, who told me that if he did not make some real changes, including committing to weekly therapy, he was going to a group home, one far away from "civilization." In the next breath she stated that he was a smart kid who had a great side to him, a side she wished to see more often.

We sat down, and I told him about confidentiality and the exceptions to it. For instance, if he were to tell me something was "going down" and where and against whom, I would have to call the police. I also told him my ground rules: He was not allowed to hurt or threaten me, hurt himself, or destroy anything in the office on purpose. Apart from that, barring safety threats to himself or others, he could use whatever language he needed to use, and I would not tell his social worker or anyone else what we talked about unless he and I discussed it beforehand and agreed on what could be said. I added one last thing: I was there to help him; I was not a teacher who would grade him on how well he did or did not do during our sessions. There was no right or wrong way to be in my office. I became quiet while Carlos continued to text on his phone with one earphone in his ear and the volume turned up so loud I had no problem hearing the music.

After about half the session had passed, I asked whether he wanted to play Uno between texts, just to make time pass a bit quicker; we both knew he had to hang out with me for 50 minutes, not just this week but once every week for the foreseeable future. He agreed to that. That became our routine: We played Uno while he also answered his texts and listened to music in one ear. I asked a question here and there: Who was the teacher he disliked the most? What was the worst thing about his foster home? My comments were focused on siding with his experience: I agreed it was not right that his foster parents would buy their daughter a big meal from McDonalds whereas he had to eat the regular dinner, and it was not right that their daughter had a TV in her room but he did not.

As we continued to see each other, Carlos became more verbal and gave me longer answers, with me being able to ask progressively deeper questions. I started to explore his involvement with the gang. It was a slow process, given that anyone involved in a gang is not prone to talking about it and also because I suspected that this was a sensitive topic in other ways as well. My questions were about how he felt when he was with his "homies": What had made him decide to affiliate himself with the gang at such a young age, and what did it mean to him that they had accepted him as one of them? He slowly started to share that he knew the other gang members were there for him; they "had his back." He always had someone to hang out and smoke with when things were too difficult around the foster home or when he just felt down. I spoke about this as support and belonging, acknowledging what he experienced as positive and that I understood his need to feel this belonging. I was well aware that all the other adults in his life told him about all the bad things that came out of being a gang member: the illegal activities, the drug use, and the danger. I told him I agreed with them but that I also understood the other side. These discussions lasted over a few months of playing Uno, a period during which he also, to my cautious delight, did less and less texting. Some time during this period the music stopped as well.

Carlos began sharing more about the opposite of the feelings of support he felt from his friends in the gang: He felt that no one else wanted him; his dad had totally dropped out of his life, his mom had moved away and was deemed by social services to be an unfit mother, and his school could not suspend him quickly enough any time he even spoke out of turn in class. He said that there was only one person he had ever felt "cared about him even some": an old boyfriend of his mom's. He had some sporadic contact with the man, who had managed to clean up his life and now worked as a counselor at a drug rehabilitation center in town.

I asked Carlos whether I could speak to the social worker about this man so that we could see whether there was a way he could come to one of the sessions and I could meet him, because he meant something to Carlos. Carlos agreed. He knew he wanted support and belonging; he did not have many people in his life whom he saw as his allies. We invited this man, and I facilitated a discussion between them about Carlos's need to have someone in his life and what it was he longed for. The ex-boyfriend was perceptive and showed interest in stepping up.

As we neared the end of Carlos's eighth-grade year, I received a voicemail from him on a Monday morning. He asked whether he could come to see me as soon as possible, even though our session was not until later that week. I called back and asked him to come in that same day. When he came to the session he sat down and started crying. He told me he had been out with one of his close friends on Saturday evening, and a few teenagers from the opposing gang had shot this friend. Carlos was not the target and got away unhurt. He called 911, and the friend was taken to the hospital with life-threatening injuries. Carlos was in shock, and what he did was to call his therapist. After a year of working together I now knew he saw me as a person whom he could seek and receive support from. This made it possible for him to share his fears about possibly being the target the next time, his fears that his friend might die, and all the images he had from that evening when he tried to stop his friend from bleeding to death.

After this experience Carlos realized he wanted to change. He started to see that what he longed for he might be able to get from someone other than his friends in the gang. He continued to be in contact with his mother's ex-boyfriend, who had been participating in some of Carlos's therapy sessions. Carlos asked his social worker whether it would be possible for him to spend weekends with this man. The social worker agreed to this arrangement. Carlos also announced that he did not want to attend the regular high school because he would only be known as the "old" Carlos he used to be. He and I checked out some of the alternative high schools and found one that seemed to be a good fit for him: a small school with few students in each class and teachers who would be there for the students even after the school day was over, a school that spoke about the importance of building community among students and adults. Again, my job as a therapist went outside the therapy room in an effort to help my client get the support he needed.

We continued our work together for 1 more year, during which I never saw the cell phone during the sessions; even the Uno game was put away. We sorted out some of the issues that had made him start using drugs, something he had more or less stopped doing during this year. He slowly started to build new friendships, friends whom he felt supported by without having to create a bond under the dire common fate of being in a gang together. Carlos now could find support in his teachers, his mother's ex-boyfriend (who was taking the steps toward becoming Carlos's guardian), and to some extent, me. His teachers reported that he was able to come to them and talk about what was bothering him instead of trying to get their attention in a negative way.

We wrapped up our sessions together after about two years, but our contact has not stopped. Carlos calls and leaves me messages from time to time telling me how his life is going. Things have generally been going well for him: He is living with his new guardian (his mom's ex-boyfriend), has 1 year left in high school, is on track to graduate, and feels generally pleased with his life. I know he knows that if something should go wrong or he is not feeling supported enough in his life, he can always come back for more sessions. His messages, I believe, are to help him keep the connection with me, to help him know he can reach out if he wants to.

DIANA: TRAUMA AND ROLLER COASTERS

The treatment of clients with trauma is a fast-growing sector within the psychotherapeutic field. Trauma is biochemically encoded in the brain (Cozolino, 2010), and the notion that the trauma is not in the event but in the nervous system makes the knowledge of neuroscience important (van der Kolk, 2006). van der Kolk (2006) pointed out that the individuals most likely to develop the symptoms of posttraumatic stress disorder (PTSD) are the ones who fail to establish a new homeostasis after a traumatic event. As relational gestalt therapists, we would say that the best way to establish a new homeostasis is by being in a relationship with someone who can provide an attuned, empathic presence and a calming sense that everything will be all right. The effect of the trauma is seen in the way the traumatic event comes to dominate the total organism and how the person organizes her or his life after the event. In Gestalt theoretical terms, a person who experiences the symptoms of trauma has a different way of perceiving his or her field after as opposed to before the traumatic event happened, an insight which is helpful in therapeutic work with these clients.

Diana, a 36-year-old Caucasian woman working as a school administrator and living with her 13-year-old son, was encouraged by her son's therapist to seek therapy for PTSD, which she had developed during years of living with a physically and emotionally abusive husband. At her first session Diana sat on the edge of the chair, hugging her purse in front of her on her lap. She avoided eye contact, her eyes darting from one point in the room to another in no seeming order. When I (LA) was first introduced to her by her son's therapist, who suggested that Diana needed her own support, Diana was reluctant to start therapy. She did not want to talk about what had happened to her but just wanted to move on. I assured her that I would not force her to talk about anything she did not feel like talking about, that she was in control over her own treatment, and that I in fact welcomed her "no" in our work and would not be offended; on the contrary, I would celebrate it. To be able to say no and have that respected by the recipient is to express your personal boundaries—exactly the boundaries that are violated in interpersonal trauma.

Just a few months earlier Diana and her son had moved from southern California to a small town in the north to get away from Diana's husband (who was her son's father). The marriage had been filled with domestic violence, and Diana had sustained physical injuries during the last few years. When her husband pushed her down the stairs and she badly injured her leg, she finally reached the point where she was able to leave the relationship.

My intention during (and after) the first session was to help Diana feel less threatened in the room with me, more able to explore trusting her present situation. I took care to let her take this at her own pace, making her own decision as to whether this was the right place for her to be at this point. The question was not whether she needed help—we both agreed on that—but whether my office was the right choice for her right now (and I the right person). The notion of control is important when working with trauma; one of the defining hallmarks of trauma is the lack of control over the situation. My intention was to show Diana that she was in control and that she could get up and leave the room at any moment, without any negative consequences (again, I would not be offended). This was exactly what she had not been able to do with her husband, through the many years of abuse.

The notion that trust is just an early stage of therapy, something we spend a bit of time building before we achieve it, is one of those notions for which a Gestalt perspective gives us a different view. From a Gestalt point of view, trust is not something you simply have or do not have; rather, it is an ongoing experiential process on a multidimensional continuum. That is, one may come to trust a person in one area under certain conditions but not in other areas or under different conditions. Trust is not a single event or a final state but a complex, dynamic interpersonal field condition, subjectively perceived (like all social field conditions) and which changes, evolves, complexifies, and perhaps deepens (or not) over time. The dynamics of trust are always there; in a Gestalt view, a major part of our role as therapists, as can be seen in these cases, is to offer supportive relational-field conditions in the session to keep deepening the safety of the here-and-now field so that the client can keep experimenting with more self-management of risk and exposure level between therapist and client. This, after all, is the capacity that is needed in every situation of life if we are to live freely and choicefully in a range of situations, as opposed to rigidly and avoidantly, or heedlessly and reactively. As always in Gestalt, we "work on" issues by exploring them actively in the here-and-now process that is our living experimental lab. *Working on* and *exploring* in Gestalt are the same: We expand capacity by knowing our own and one another's process better, not by trying to "fix" it.

For victims of abuse, especially if the perpetrator was a person with whom the victim had a close relationship, the concept of trust becomes difficult and likely generalized: How can I trust anybody around me if the person I trusted and let in hurt me so? Paradoxically, the closer I get to a new person now, the more anxious I may become about trust, because I now have more exposure and more to lose. How can I trust my own judgment about whom to trust at all, if I have been so wrong in the past?

As we continued to talk about Diana's day-to-day life and what her interests were, she started to slowly relax; she put down her purse, and I could tell her breathing had slowed, signaling to me that her nervous system was becoming less hyperaroused. At that point I directed her attention to the sensations in her body and how she felt being in the room with me at that moment. She reported that she felt a bit calmer and that it was easier to breathe, but at this point she still was not able to report any body sensations.

Thus, our first experiment (still managed by me in this early stage because she was not ready yet for a full therapeutic partnership in the usual sense) was supporting her and waiting for her to be able to "show up in the room." When she could register sensations in her own body, I would know that her reactive dissociation response to the years of abuse in which she had become paralyzed had begun to ebb, at least in our sessions. At that stage we began having conversations about the daily issues and struggles she and her son were experiencing: relocating, their loss of financial stability, living with PTSD (meaning, for Diana, learning how to be around more than just a few people at a time), Diana's deep concern about her son's well-being following the suicide attempts that had brought him—and then her—into counseling, and her positive longing, under all that, for a future in which she felt in control of her own life. As we talked, I kept gently inviting her to start noticing her body—specifically simple, concrete sensations. I slowed down the process to help her titrate the hyperarousal she often experienced, offering her the simple experiment of looking at my face to see whether that was calming her or making her nervous; this quickly became a new source of support for her. Much of my attention was on her nervous system arousal (again, as indicated by her breathing or other signs of agitation), supporting her to find and practice ways of regulating her nervous system both in the sessions with me and on her own outside the sessions.

As Diana began reporting that her life was feeling more "under control," she felt more able to handle day-to-day living, and she also began to speak about the abuse she had lived through with her ex-husband. I was not pushing her in that direction; it was something she was ready to do on her own "organically" because she felt supported enough by our relationship and the self-regulating skills she was gradually mastering. At this point in our work together she could identify her own sensations when she felt anxious or fearful, and we both worked together on managing this new level of physical awareness as she learned to slow down the process so she did not become overwhelmed.

When Diana expressed feelings of anger at her ex-husband, instead of using a hesitant, deadened voice, she spoke from a place of greater strength (being "in her power," Diana called it) and not from the place of a frightened victim. Both her body posture and her tone were different. This gave me the sense she was ready to tolerate a higher level of arousal: From this place I invited her to fantasize about what she could imagine doing to him as "payback." This was challenging. Gathering her strength visibly, she spoke in a calm, determined voice. She imagined having him strapped in a roller coaster for some hours without a break—she knew he "hates roller coasters and is afraid of heights." Just that: not violence but being trapped in fear. Suddenly she started to laugh, and I laughed with her. The perfect payback: just a taste of what she had felt living with him; no physical damage, no direct pain, but now he would know. Her comment at this point was that she did not know which felt better: the freedom to imagine the perfect revenge or our shared space to laugh about it together.

After this landmark conversation, Diana felt centered in a different, freer place. With this much self-regulation in place, we "brought" her ex-husband into the office—not in person but in the form of an empty chair. At first this was just to see how Diana felt imagining being in the same room with him without saying anything, but she soon found the power in herself to start giving voice to all the things she had been too afraid to tell him when they lived together and he abused her. At this point in the therapy she was well aware of the sensations in her body and her arousal level; whenever she started to feel a higher level of charge, she would track herself and slow down the process or turn to me and say that she felt a bit overwhelmed and needed help to ground herself again. Her life, she told me, was "opening back up." She felt, as she put it, "like my old self again."

ARMINDA AND SAM: LONELINESS AND INTIMACY

"It's just that I'd rather be lonely by myself, than go on being lonely with you." Because Arminda had already told me (GW) on the phone when she booked the appointment that she and her husband needed help "negotiating the divorce," I was not completely taken aback by these bleak words. Still, we both turned to Sam, whose face I read as glum, somewhere between resentful, hopeless, and exhausted. Silence, followed by more silence.

"Tell me something about what you're experiencing right now, when Arminda says that," I finally offered. I put it this way in hopes of getting something fresher than a prepared answer but also to test out and begin modeling a practice I imagined was probably missing in their relationship: If Arminda was this lonely after some 25 years of marriage and family life, it seemed unlikely that they had much facility or even capacity to share their real inner experience with each other—or perhaps to know it themselves.

"Well it's not like she hasn't said it before," Sam offered after another long pause. "And your reaction?" I queried again. "Don't see the point of it," Sam spoke in a tired voice. "I don't want to be alone, at this age." They were both close to 60. "And after all that trouble it would probably just not be that different with another person." With that pronouncement Sam lapsed back into his slumped, withdrawn state.

This was one of the occasions for which here-and-now experience as a therapist is so key to the process. Already after a couple of remarks I began to feel how lonely it might be to live with this man, who I also knew, from Arminda's initial conversation, was a "good father," "a good man," "good in a crisis," "a good provider," and who had several other good qualities as well. The question was what to do with my own feelings, which could easily be experienced by Sam as accusatory, "siding with her" from the beginning, and likely critical and shaming as well. At the same time I felt sadness thinking of how lonely Sam must be and imagining that his loneliness might well just be "like water to the fish," something so deeply constant and habitual he was not fully aware of any other way to be. To flood him with possibly overwhelming, possibly intrusive empathy that may have seemed condescending might have made me one more problematic person to be managed in some way. I decided to take a different kind of risk: "I guess my problem here—and maybe you can help me with this—is that I don't really believe you."

This jolted Sam out of his hangdog look. "Oh, I don't mean I think you're lying," I hastened to add. "I'm sure what you said is true—divorce is a lot of trouble and so is dating, or whatever it is you're thinking would come after that. But I'm looking at your face—I believe I see a lot of sadness, and I'm thinking after 25 years, with grown children doing well, a lot of life ahead to share together—or not. And that's when I don't believe you when you say the reason you don't want to divorce is just that it would be a lot of trouble."

"OK, touché," said Sam with a rueful smile and a bit more engagement. Then he added, "But actually, I didn't say that was the reason." I became mock-judicious, suppressing a smile. "No, you didn't say 'the.' Point taken." That exchange set the tone for Sam's and my relationship: He was going to allow, even reluctantly welcome, my pushing him beyond his comfort zone, as long as we could still engage in a friendly poke back and forth to reestablish parity on the terrain of humor and verbal intelligence.

I have drawn this out a bit to illustrate how critical it is to establish some equal-weight alliance with each partner, if couples therapy is to be productive. In this case, Arminda was a primary grades teacher, I am a therapist, and Sam was a successful engineer. The territory Arminda wanted to explore and claim was *intimacy*—that transparent, unguarded, and authentic sharing of our inner thoughts, feelings, and states of being—which is something gender typed more as feminine than masculine in the crude stereotypes of North American culture. For all these reasons I paid special attention to finding and supporting a kind of contact with Sam—slightly sparring, perhaps more "male-typed"—that he could feel comfortable and "in charge" with, before moving to challenge his habitual ways of feeling safe in relationships, which were leaving Arminda in such a lonely place.

What is intimacy from a Gestalt perspective? What does it do for us when we know how to experience and transact it? Why can it be so desperately painful when we do not have it—especially in close relationships of couples, families, and other connections in which that longing comes up so easily and so often? The answer to this question hearkens back to our Gestalt understanding of human development, experience, and behavior. Behavior, our model tells us, emerges as a best-available, constructed response to some challenge—originally, the challenge of how to satisfy our needs for attachment, nourishment, safety, and some degree of emotional resonance in earliest infancy and then all through childhood. As we cocreate strategies and solutions for these developmental and survival challenges, which originally occurred in our families, we are constantly habituating our responses so that most of our behavior becomes automatic, while we turn present, active attention to the constantly new challenges at hand.

As we discussed earlier and have illustrated in these cases, these complex habit responses can be flexible and open to further learning and development, or they may be more rigid "emergency" responses girded with anxiety boundaries that make them resistant to further change and growth. These become parts of the stuck areas of our lives. What makes the difference between these two kinds of development: open and creative and ever-changing, leading us to new challenges, learning, and meanings, or stuck and repetitive and unsatisfying, when "after all these years" some painful situation reoccurs and we try to deal with it (often without realizing it) in the same dysfunctional, unsatisfying way (which may have been our best possible creative solution in the past but is sadly out of date now)?

The answer, as we have seen, lies in the field conditions of support (in the past and then, at least potentially, in new situations and relationships). This is what Gestalt therapy—and perhaps all therapy—is about: promoting and providing a new safe container and a supportive relationship that can serve as the experimental field for feeling and opening up these old habit chains that may have been long out of awareness and too protected by anxiety reactions (or worse, in severe trauma, including panic attacks, dissociation, or even violent responses toward others or the self). This is Goodman's idea of therapy as a "safe emergency," a venue for "proximal learning" (Zaretskii, 2009): These are safe enough for the client to relax some of the old anxiety and mobilization, and at the same time they have just enough "real life" urgency to support using the "lab" of the therapeutic relationship as a venue for trying out new behaviors and new supports (in the session or as "homework" the client and therapist designs together) or, more simply and organically, by attending to the ongoing "experiment" of contact in the therapy session and in the relationship.

As we come back to again and again in this volume and in Gestalt theory and practice, our method for providing that safe container and that supportive field for exploration is first and foremost by "showing up" with the most fully attuned, empathic, and authentic presence we can provide. Contemporary neuroscience has confirmed and expands on the notion every day that when we do this, our fuller activation of "integrated brain circuitry" (Siegel, 2010) has effects on the client's sense of resources and (relative) relaxation, supporting new awareness and the opening up of old patterns long locked in anxiety and reactivity so that change can begin to take place.

However, this same supportive container, permitting the relaxation of old blocks and facilitating new growth in relationships, can exist outside therapy, potentially any time we are in a sustained relationship with a friend or partner who can show up empathically in this (e.g., C. M. Wilson

& Oswald, 2005). In other words, intimacy (whether in marriage or other emotionally intimate relationships) is not a luxury for the benefit of a privileged few; rather, an intimate relationship (whether in a couple or with close friends) is an ongoing support for the growth of personal and relational capacities and meaning making throughout life. This is why intimacy, in this full, emotionally resonant and empathic sense, is so important in life and only becomes more so as we grow older.

We repeatedly find that those areas of life in which one can feel that empathic gaze, that acceptance and curious interest from important others, and that sense of available support are the areas of life that have kept growing and developing flexibly and openly, leading one in widening and deepening circles of complex understanding, relationships, and creativity. Conversely, areas of life in which that has been missing, or worse (where one has been met with shaming or worse abuse), tend to be the areas in which something in life feels stuck; the same old patterns come around painfully again and again and disappointment often makes one avoid that area altogether. In other words, the intimate regard of the other—that empathic interest and seeing and wanting to know what's going on "inside me" for its own sake (i.e., not just strategically to get me to do something)—is the key field support for stimulating, unblocking, and supporting growth in any area of life (including therapy); this is true not just in childhood but at any time all through our lives.

This was exactly the kind of process Arminda and Sam were so handicapped in transacting: the capacity to offer empathic interest and curiosity about what was going on with each other, where their thoughts and feelings and behavior were coming from, how they were perceiving and feeling (and fearing and hoping about) the world. Arminda and Sam had lost the capacity to trust and welcome interest from the other person and make use of it to know themselves better and thus become freer, less reactive, more responsive, and more able to meet each situation as it arose, with its unique challenges and opportunities, so that they could respond in a fresh, more authentic, and perhaps more satisfying way.

I decided, with the security of that small moment, that little joking verbal tussle between us, as a guide, that Sam might tolerate—and Arminda could benefit from witnessing—one more small risky experiment. "So in other words," I dropped to a serious tone again and looked him full in the eyes, "Arminda is not the only one here who is lonely." Sam's eyes filled with tears, which he nervously daubed at. "The thing is . . . ," he tried to begin, but had to clear his throat, "the thing is, I don't know why that makes me cry." "Maybe to tell us all we're touching a tender area," I spoke quietly. "Maybe we can get to know a lot more about tender areas, together here, for both of you—not just to solve something, but for its own sake. For your own sakes." Then we all let the moment rest in stillness a bit longer. This is what intimacy is, after all: that warm, interested gaze (in both directions, both of us looking "into" me and then the same for you). That was what Arminda and Sam had such a hard time doing—and were about to divorce because of.

Arminda and Sam's marriage had gone well overall. Now, with less pressure, more leisure, and a new chapter of life opening up, for the first time they were "face to face," and that is where their skills and capacities were failing them. Sam had had a distant, critical father who probably wanted the best for his son but seemed to believe that the best support for that outcome would be constant coercion and correction, not just of Sam's actions (he was an achiever, but his father could still find fault) but also of his thinking, his feelings, his sullen moods or passive manner. As he grew up, Sam learned to go inward, concentrating on academics and problem solving, and just "blanked out" (his words) his thoughts and desires. If he expressed them, they would only be criticized and corrected all the more.

Arminda's parents were both more focused on their own careers than on their daughter; what time and attention they did have for their children went to her brother (ironically, considering that, in her way, her mother was a pioneering woman in her field for her day—but that meant that in the family, above all, "mom's career came first"). This legacy had given Arminda a great capacity to focus on and empathize with others, which had served her and her young students well in her own career as a teacher, but it had also given her a great need for listening, mirroring, and taking interest in her own thoughts, feelings, and experiences in an intimate relationship. The inability to feel this with Sam was so painful for her, we quickly found in the sessions, that she flipped quickly to cover her own feelings with criticism, driving him further into the adaptive withdrawal and "blankness" he had adopted under stress and criticism since childhood.

In other words, as with so many distressed couples we see, Arminda and Sam found themselves in a perfect storm of self-reinforcing conditions, a vicious circle in which the more alone Arminda felt, the more she criticized Sam, both to cover her own feelings and, in her words in those early weeks, "to assert myself, not go under—just feel myself, hear the sound of my own voice." The more criticized Sam felt, and the more he felt himself unable to "be different" and relieve her distress, the more he withdrew, "waiting for it to blow over." The thousand tasks and even the crises of family life came as a relief to him because these were problems he could share with her and they could work on together. Without those problems, he felt depressed, hopeless, and helpless to change.

Sam and Arminda were sophisticated, highly verbal people. As young adults they had known each other's parents, and each had quite a bit of empathy for what the other one was "up against," now and especially as a child. This close knowledge of the other (and of the self) in the moment, and especially under stress, was new to them. The idea that their contact styles, especially in emotional conflict, were an amalgam of old habit responses learned under high stress and low support made immediate sense to them verbally, but they had no idea how to apply this in the heat of the moment. Together in the sessions we learned to identify the stress adaptation for each of them. Sam's first impulse was to look for a problem he could solve. Failing that, he went into the withdrawal that was dulling him and panicking Arminda. Arminda was aware of "filling the space with the sound of my own voice" to forestall a feeling of disappearing and becoming totally invisible, which she could directly relate to her childhood. She had some idea of how critical she sounded but did not realize how that was affecting Sam (not surprising, because he was doing his utmost to cover up his own feelings, even from himself).

Completely new to them was the idea of "dropping down" to look for the deeper feelings covered by habitual adaptation and then speaking from there. Over the weeks, they learned to recognize the top impulse (to assert or criticize or to withdraw or "go blank"—admittedly a harder one to "catch in the act," as Sam put it). Because Sam particularly wanted concrete cues, we worked out that any time Arminda spoke from "below" the criticism (naming any vulnerable feeling, such as feeling alone, wanting his companionship, needing to feel seen, and the like), he would likewise reach for some true feeling and offer it at "more than three-word length" (his words). The keys to this kind of more intimate exchange are (a) to remember that any offering of authentic experience such as this is a gift and (b) in case of hesitation, one can always go with the actual here-and-now experience (which at that moment, is the hesitation), as in, for example, "Right now I'm not sure what to say because I'm afraid I'll say it badly or it could easily be misinterpreted," and so forth.

This kind of close attention to emotional process is Gestalt contact work opened up. It is also the flow of intimacy in vivo for couples and others, the enacting of a fuller personal presence that keeps a nourishing exchange going, providing the emotional base for all the changes and challenges a couple faces all through life (even when some of the earlier life tasks have been handled successfully, as here). Elements of this kind of feeling exchange may take place and be facilitative in any relationship; where knowing the other (and the self) is a goal for its own sake, the relationship becomes an intimate one, symmetrically intimate in a friendship or equal couple but also appropriately asymmetrical, at least to a degree, in caretaking and facilitative relationships such as parent–child, teacher–student, or therapist–client (all cases where a fully equal "equal-time" process would be burdensome and developmentally inappropriate for the client, student, or child). This is not because a client is in an infantilized position but rather because the client's position is especially privileged in terms of the agenda and contract that bring the parties together.

In all these cases the full, interested, and empathic presence of one partner becomes the facilitative field conditions for exploration and growth for the other (and for the self—giving these conditions is as powerful a change–intervention for the self as it is for the recipient). Going back to our basic Gestalt understanding of contact as creative problem solving (adaptation) often followed by automation or habitual patterning of the adaptation, we can see where the facilitative, inquiring presence of one leads to the relaxation of too-rigid habits in the other and the opportunity to experiment together on a freer and more satisfying new adaptation (leading to a new habit practice). In this way intimate relationships—those in which intimate process in this sense becomes a goal not just strategically but in its own right—whether as couples or as intimate friends or relations, are our natural relational lab for ongoing personal growth and development throughout life. Thus, in this Gestalt relational sense, intimate relationships become the ongoing venue and life-lab for growth in depth and freedom of awareness and choice, just as the process works in therapy. In the words often attributed to the systemic thinker Gregory Bateson (1979), "It takes two to know one." With this insight, plus the new skills to back it up and put it in action, Arminda and Sam had a new opportunity to make the new chapter of their already long marriage into a challenging, rewarding, and evolving new adventure.

DAISY: JUMP ROPE AND JUNGLE GYM

Violet Oaklander (2006) wrote, "Children come to therapy for two basic reasons: for one, they have difficulty making good contact: contact with teachers, parents, peers, books. Secondly, they generally have a poor sense of self" (p. 5). Daisy, a 9-year-old Hispanic girl, was referred to therapy by her teacher. She lived with her parents and three younger brothers, with her extended family close by. Daisy was morbidly obese and had poor social skills, general anxiety, and low academic performance; thus, she seemed to fit Oaklander's picture well. She was seen through a school-based program for low-income students, which gave them the opportunity to receive free therapy at their school during school hours (for some families this may often be the only way we have of being sure the child can show up for the therapy session).

I (LA) have a toy magic wand in the playroom that Daisy found during our first session, no doubt because I often put it in a strategic place when I meet with a client for the first time. When she found it, I asked her what three things she would like to change in her life if she could have three wishes come true. First, she wished she could play like the other kids during recess—and that they would want to play with her. Her second wish was that her father would stop drinking all those beers and yelling at her mother, her brother, and her. Her third wish was to not feel so scared all the time. I responded that I could help her with the first and the third wish but that the second one was more difficult because her dad was not the one coming to my office to play with me, she was. She agreed that made some sense.

As she continued to explore my office this first session, I invited her to play, and it soon became clear that she did not know how even to begin. I suggested we make up a story in the sand tray together, but when we tried this, Daisy would just put one or two figurines in the sand, say one sentence, and then become stuck. She moved from one activity to the next without settling. As we tossed the ball to each other I was saddened, but not surprised, to notice her poor motor skills.

Toward the end of our first session I noticed that Daisy had a bossy way of relating to me, which actually made me want to finish the session before our 50 minutes were up. She asked me to get things from the shelf when she was sitting at the table instead of getting up and getting them herself. If I said that she could do it herself, she responded that she did not want to but instead wanted me to do it for her. When it was time to clean up after an activity, she told me to do it while she started looking for the next thing to do. I gently told her that we were both responsible for cleaning up. She reluctantly helped but did it so slowly that I ended up doing most of the cleaning myself. Because it was our first session, I told myself this was something we would slowly work on; if this was her opening style with a total stranger, I could only assume it was a pervasive pattern in her life.

After our first session I reflected on what I had observed in Daisy's play (or rather, lack of play) and her lack of gross motor skills and body awareness, along with the uncomfortable feeling I was left with. Given the myriad issues that had been mentioned in the referral and that I had observed during the session, I decided to take a somewhat more directive approach than with most other clients, working mostly with the issue she mentioned as her first wish: to be able to play like the other children. My hope was that we would then also be able to address some of her anxiety, her lack of social skills, and then, if and as she started to feel a better sense of herself, to build what we could call self-esteem.

As we started to work together, I scheduled her sessions when there was no recess, which meant we had the playground at our disposal. I brought a jump rope and a ball. We would toss the ball while we checked in on how her week had been, and then we started practicing with the jump rope. Daisy had never tried it before even though this was a popular activity during recess among the girls in her class. Her poor self-esteem became evident immediately: She told me she could not do it, so she was not even going to try. I told her that everyone starts from not knowing how to jump rope and that no one but me would see if she could not do it. I asked her how she would feel if she could jump rope like the girls in her class, to give her the chance to refocus on a positive feeling. She agreed to try, with little success, but with me as the most enthusiastic cheerleader she could ever have. As we took turns jumping, I asked what she could tell herself as she practiced to make her feel better about herself. She came up with, "Never give up, keep trying." As we continued our work together, that became our mantra, a sentence Daisy started using in different situations outside our sessions to help her get over her impulse to give up as soon as something got a little bit more difficult.

We also used the playground to do other physical experiments because Daisy was longing to be able to climb the jungle gym. As anticipated, her anxiety was high, and I helped her learn to use her breathing and her attention to focus on her body, tracking (not fixing) how her anxiety felt. She said it was like butterflies in her stomach, so I proposed she try picturing the butterflies flying out of her stomach when she exhaled, taking her anxiety with them. With practice this was something else that helped her, and we slowly started progressing.

With her obesity, her stamina for physical activities was limited, so our sessions were usually split between a more active first half outside and the second half in the playroom. I would follow Daisy's lead during this part of the session but gently tell her how I felt about her way of treating me when I felt pushed around. My intention was to show her that I would not leave her but that I had feelings about how I was treated—that is, I was not a nonentity; we were both people with feelings, and she was having an impact on me. I told her I absolutely needed her to help clean up before moving on to the next activity, something she quickly got better at. She liked art, and as she drew I would ask her questions to help her elaborate on what she was drawing or painting: What happened next? How did the dog feel? What did the boy want to tell his mom? Open questions such as these, in the context of our relationship and her sense of my real interest, began to offer a reparative field where her imagination could grow.

As Daisy's play slowly began to give me a sense that she was stretching and using her imagination and creativity, we were able to start to play in the dollhouse with the puppets and sometimes in the sand tray. I used my sense of being in relation to her as my guide for working with her, and then I used the relational Gestalt stance of reflecting back my own reactions: I wanted her to be able to state what she wanted and direct the play, but if my body began to feel reactive, I allowed myself to listen and give voice to it. For example, I would make a comment about how I was starting to feel left out and as if she just wanted to be the one deciding everything, which did not make it fun to play with her. If she was telling my puppet to do something scary, I would state as the puppet that I felt scared and anxious, giving her the chance to be in the comforting role, counseling me to take a deep breath to let the butterflies fly away.

As we continued finding our way to greater contact together, Daisy slowly began to change outside our sessions as well. Her teacher reported that she was doing better academically, and she participated more in the classroom activities. I could observe on the playground how she started slowly, step by step, to join in with the other girls, first on the outside but after a few months making a best friend. It was a delight to see the two girls "connected at the hip" during recess, playing on the playground or sitting on a bench just talking. Daisy started expressing how much she liked coming to school and how it had become a refuge from her home life. Meanwhile, not from lack of trying on my part, family life had not changed for Daisy, and my sense was that it likely would not. Her parents had turned down all the invitations for collateral sessions with a family therapist. At least Daisy and I, in almost a full school year, had together created one part of her life where she felt safe and happy.

During the following 2 years before Daisy moved on to middle school she and I would check in from time to time—a few times about issues with other girls and sometimes just for her to have someone to share her successes with. As with many of the clients in this school-based program, Daisy did not just need to be seen and heard when things were not going well; she needed as much for her successes to be seen and heard. Providing this kind of "mirroring field," lacking in Daisy's family as in so many others, had served to put Daisy back on a path of her own development. She transitioned to middle school with more capacity to weather the even heavier developmental storms and challenges ahead.

JASON: NEGOTIATING THE THERAPIST'S OWN SHAME ISSUES

As a gay man who came of age, painfully and courageously, in the 1970s and 1980s, Jason was well-acquainted with shame as an experience and shaming as a dynamic—both were actively dealt to him by others and then later on, as will almost inevitably happen after heavy early shaming, as a learned contact adaptation, a stuck self-contacting style. I (GW) reflected and we experimented and talked about this harsh way of relating to himself and others as a reflexive and protective habit ("I'll beat up on myself before you can do it") and also as a sad child's way of bringing the critical parents and others closer and feeling less alone ("I'm like you; we're close because we both beat up on me"). He had never suffered physical or sexual abuse at home (although he did experience both outside the home as a teenager), but the disapproval, even revulsion, from his father about his "sissiness" (his father's word) had long hung over his life. The effect of all this had been a profound sense of self-shame and "wrongness" holding him back from moving ahead in relationships and career. After several years of therapy, Jason had made profound changes in both these areas of life, and he was well able to talk about his own issues of shame.

We had talked from the beginning about the profound experiment he was conducting—a first for him after a series of gay therapists—by engaging in the intimate process of therapy with a straight man, thus inviting all kinds of assumptions and projections on his part about me, my attitudes about sexuality in general and his sexuality in particular, and his anticipation of revulsion on my part (like his father's) at hearing about his specific sexual preferences and fantasies. To have his sexuality seen, affirmed, and celebrated by an older man with a different sexual identity from his own was transformational to Jason. On the strength of it, he was able to experiment outside therapy with critical conversations with his elderly father, asking him point-blank why he had been so hard on Jason in his younger years; his father, despite being in the early stages of dementia, was still able to answer that he had seen his own role as requiring him to "toughen up" Jason, partly protectively and partly for reasons, his father confessed, that "I just don't know myself." Jason had tears in his eyes as he told me of the flood of affirmation he felt from this moment of frankness, regret, and respect between two very different men. I had tears in my eyes listening to him, silently thanking the universe and his father for finding the resources to come forward and meet him in that healing way. Contact, as we can see from this brief moment, does not have to be in agreement with what may have been desired; it does not have to be perfect and without flaws to be transformational—it only has to be authentic, generous-hearted, and a direct person-to-person meeting.

Meanwhile, Jason was changing his life. He moved out of an unaffirming, non-nourishing relationship into exploring others that were new and different, and he moved out of assistant jobs into full management, where he was able to hold his own in a new way in contact, and at times conflict, with a diverse and challenging range of people. Thus, it took me by surprise when he came in one day in a deep funk. "Same old, same old," he lamented. "Nothing ever changes—I've got the same old issues and problems I had before I ever started this whole process. I'm insecure, I'm not at ease with people, I don't get respect, I'm not attractive. I'm hopeless, and I just better give up."

Instead of resonating with this wave of shame and then perhaps inquiring about the triggers for it, I reminded Jason instead how much better he had been feeling for some time now. He countered that he always fell back, that all his work had been for nothing. I reframed by telling him that he was meeting some of the same issues, but he was meeting them in a much more demanding context, taking on much more bold and challenging situations than he was able to before, even if these new challenges were sometimes daunting. His hopelessness only deepened. And so it went, back and forth, in a kind of spiraling-down argument, where each reassurance from me was met with more self-blaming and shaming and finally a kind of despair. At some point I snapped out of it and broke it off, appealing to the "contact consultant" we always have with us in the session: the client him- or herself. What was I doing here and now, I inquired, that was contributing to this downward spiral? Where was I missing him? Jason's first response (now he moved to reassure me) was that it was not me at all, it was him. I had been nothing but supportive and available; he was the one who was just too defective to make use of all this support.

What had happened to worsen such a sharp decline? I moved to take the contact sequence apart. "You came in feeling bad," I reviewed, "and I moved immediately into what must have felt like trying to talk you out of it." "No, no, you were really nice," Jason protested weakly. "Yeah, nice," I said, reaching deeper, "but still sort of telling you why you shouldn't be feeling what you were feeling—something you've had more than enough of in your life already, in too many ways. All I can come up with right now"—I went on reaching deeper into myself—"is that something about your coming in that way must have triggered a feeling in me that I'm not doing enough. If you're feeling that low, after all this therapy, then I must not be much of a therapist; I should be doing more." "You could say I'm acting like your father used to," I went on. "You were a kid, you had a problem—and if you told him about it, you had two problems." For the first time, Jason's breathing slowed and deepened; he even hazarded a smile. "So if you're having a hard time, I'm a failure, and then you have to start reassuring me. Somehow your shame is triggering mine, and if I'm not in touch with that, it turns into your problem." From there, by finding and owning the problem in my own process, we could both open up and return to considering his.

"Fixing," reassuring, and even positively reframing at certain moments are all delicate moves that can easily break the contact, positioning the therapist as the sharply defined expert and making whatever is happening in the room into the client's problem. Thus, meeting shame with "you really shouldn't be feeling that way" is always potentially isolating and always risks sounding like "you should just get over it"; to that extent it can only be reshaming. At times, in our heartfelt distress in the face of our client's distress, we can easily fall into this "contact trap," all the more easily if some shame feelings of our own ("I'm inadequate to this task; I'm not doing enough here") are triggered, and we are not fully aware of it. The cure for this problem is taking simple ownership of these feelings, modeling that the therapist can make a mistake, miss a cue, or have an issue, and still be all right, still be whole, and still be committed and available to the client. In fact, I am all the more available at that point, because I have taken back the responsibility that is mine, which is something Jason never got from his own father until near the end.

As with every intervention in Gestalt, there is no "one size fits all," no universal application of any particular specific move. With a client with less self-coherence or less history between us, I could have "owned" the same problem inside my mind while sharing much less of myself. I might simply say, for example, "I think I didn't stop to fully receive what you were feeling and telling me before I moved into some action. Let's go back, and with your help we'll try that again." The particular move is created for the here-and-now moment out of the present contact situation, but it derives from the general Gestalt principle that we shift from the content to the contact process and share that shift with as much or as little personal transparency as serves that client at that time as best we can judge it. Always remember at least to consider asking the client how the exchange went, how it felt, what hopes or fears or feelings it confirmed or—at times productively—contradicted.

ADRIANA: SHAME AND THE IMPORTANCE OF COMMUNITY

Gestalt perspective, as we have seen, is founded on the unique creativity of each human being and on our deep interconnectedness to our social field of belonging, interaction, challenges, and meanings. These two qualities— creative uniqueness and deep relationality—define us as human beings. In Gestalt perspective it is impossible, ultimately, to reduce us only to our social group of belonging and meaning, and it is equally impossible to extract us wholly from that socially codetermined human process of cocreation and coconstruction of behavior, self-definition, and meaning making. We are never completely independent of our social reference groups, and we are never just "the same as" those groups (or any one group or subset of those groups). Our essential nature and need to belong in some meaningful way and our inherent nature and need to generate a unique experience and unique responses are both givens of our nature. Human nature, experience, and behavior emerge from the dynamic interplay of these two inherent dimensions, both social and individual, neither an isolated individual nor just a "cog" in a social machine, but something more complexly emergent out of this dynamic. These are fundamental principles of Gestalt perspective on human behavior and human experience and of Gestalt therapy theory and method.

Especially when working with clients from a different culture than our own, the Zen concept of *shoshin*—beginner's mind—having an openness, eagerness, and lack of preconceptions on any topic—in this case, our client's world of cultural meanings and allegiances—is useful even when we believe we know the client's culture well. We may make use of our general knowledge of the client's culture but at the same time keep our openness to the individual in front of us with our phenomenological stance, which tells us that we cannot know how the other person is feeling or what he or she is thinking until we enter fully into that exploratory dialogue that is the essence of therapy. We attune to an emotional resonance—joy, sadness, anger, grief, excitement, fear, quiet pride, or muffled despair—which becomes full empathy only by joining with that dialogic knowing that comes from an intimate conversation based on true exploration, true openness to the pains or riches, the shocks and the hidden, perhaps healing, connections we find through discovering with the client her or his inner world of meanings.

In the following case example, 11-year-old Adriana and her family of Mixtec ethnicity, originally from the region stretching from Oaxaca to Puebla in Mexico, faced a crisis that both shook the family's cohesion and threatened (in their view) their essential membership in their own primary cultural group. Their culture was not a textbook stereotype of Hispanic, Catholic, or even first-generation Hispanic. Nor was it Mexican, again an assumptive generalization (including well-intentioned texts that sometimes give generic descriptions). The literature tells us that Mixtec is a culture (again, this is an assumption that we cannot know is true in this specific case until we engage in a dialogue with the client to see whether it holds true for her) in which the sense of community welfare and well-being is so strong as to override the individual's or even the particular family's interest. This tendency becomes even stronger when members of this Mesoamerican group immigrate to the United States, where they may be a looked-down-on minority even within a larger disadvantaged population of Mexican and other Hispanic first-generation immigrant workers. Catholic faith is likely to be strong, and with that there may be a tension between the pressure to conform to strong norms of behavior and a duty to protect and care for children in the disordered and relatively unregulated social environment in which these particular families find themselves.

Within this complex dynamic setting, the family came into the clinic in crisis. They had just discovered through their medical clinic that unbeknownst to anyone, including Adriana herself, she was pregnant and only 3 months from full term. Adriana was completely unable to account for how this had happened. Sheltered and emotionally young for her age, she was unable to name who the father might be; it was clear that she did not even know how babies were made. In her confused, minimally articulate way, she was quite adamant that she had not experienced any violent assault. Because she could not name any possible father, and because she spent little time on her own outside school, the family had been told that their daughter would have to be removed from the home, where she was likely unsafe—at least pending an investigation by social services.

The first thing that stood out about the family was their strong sense of shame about this situation. Adriana's parents did not believe that their innocent 11-year-old girl had done anything to "lead any man on," as they expressed it; they did not question Adriana's account that she honestly did not know how it had happened. Even so, a pervasive sense of shame hung over the whole family, including Adriana herself, a shame that made it difficult for the parents to participate in the investigation into who had been her abuser and was now the biological father of her child.

There was no question in their minds that the baby, when it arrived, would be placed for adoption. The question was where Adriana would go in the meantime. She could not stay at home pending the conclusion of the investigation into her abuser's identity and whether she was safe from further incidents in the family home. The recommendation of social services that she be placed with some other family member—a grandmother or an aunt (both of which she had in the community)—filled the parents with something like terror. Placing the girl with a relative would necessarily mean telling that person the reason and that would mean that their whole community would inevitably come to know about it. Adriana was therefore placed in foster care, but she was allowed to spend time with her mother and younger sister whenever possible.

In some other cultural setting the parents' reaction might be interpreted by the therapist as uncaring: Why should this young, naïve girl not be placed with a known and trusted extended family member for the duration of what to her must be a confusing, at times frightening, ordeal? It was essential to understand that, for this family, already feeling as isolated and embattled as they did in the larger Hispanic and Anglo community around them, the idea of the violation of their own small community's strict Catholic rules and norms around sexuality was not just a question of disapproval or malicious gossip; they felt the family's very survival to be at stake. A breach of their own community norms of this kind, they were convinced, would mean the end of not just the parents' but also their children's ability to live, work, worship, survive, and belong in a hostile and alien larger society.

This kind of understanding can never come from texts and programs about the content of cultural diversity in various communities. Powerful nuances and overriding emotions such as these can be appreciated and worked with only through the kind of dialogue Gestalt (along with some other methods) supports and advocates—itself based on those fundamental Gestalt precepts that we have been emphasizing in this book: Behavior is mediated by personal meanings, which are a complex emergent creation out of cultural, personal, and situational factors and dynamics; a client's inner world of meanings (as well as our own, ultimately) becomes known more clearly to therapist and client alike through a process of open exploration, experimenting, and dialogue.

After the first visit at the clinic, the therapist offered to see Adriana at school. Many of the clients at the agency were seen at their school during the school day, and each school in the district even had a therapy room set up for this purpose. The parents emphatically declined this arrangement, insisting that the mother would take Adriana to the agency, even though that meant driving from their small community to the larger town in the area, picking Adriana up at the foster home and taking her to the agency, rearranging work schedules, and paying for gas with money they did not have. All this so that the people in their community would not know that Adriana was receiving services and start to ask questions. They realized all too well that when a child is pulled out of class for appointments, confidentiality is always questionable.

In addition, the parents absolutely refused to meet with investigators or others at their home, even though both of them worked full time. The therapists involved were convinced that the parents were not trying to hide anything except the whole situation from their own community. The same issue came up in relation to the sheriff's investigation of the case as well. Viewing these challenges in this more contextual, closely attentive cross-cultural way, the therapists on the case went to work to "psychoeducate" social services and sheriff alike on the particular, uniquely complex situation of the family and their small Mesoamerican refugee community, in the context of the very different, much more disorderly, and even dangerous context they were in (including in some areas, gang activity of two and even three generations' standing). After some persuasion and advocacy on the part of the family therapist, the sheriff's department was willing to meet the family at the fire station, the closest official building in this rural area for interviews, instead of at the home as they would ordinarily have done.

Adriana asked whether her mother might bring her 2-year-old sister to her therapy sessions. Adriana explained that she felt "too lonely" in the playroom without anyone from her family there with her; at the same time the toddler was so young that her presence was not inhibiting to the therapeutic conversation. As we built our relationship and that conversation, Adriana explored for the first time her own notions about what life (i.e., middle school, her next big upcoming step) might hold and what her own needs, dreams, and desires might be. We could view this creative flexibility around the parameters of the therapy hour as another example of cultural sensitivity by the therapist, or we could see it as simply an enactment of our Gestalt principle of building support for emergent new contact. Either way, where new contact boundaries, new life challenges, new kinds of life experiments are occurring, Gestalt theory points us toward conditions of support facilitating the new adaptations life will require. In Adriana's case, some of those needed new supports involved the therapy sessions, whereas others involved, as we have seen, a deep openness on the part of the therapists to listen to this family and respond creatively, empathically, and inventively to the contextual supports that promised the most protection, healing, and care even when those arrangements differed from what we might have assumed if we simply viewed the family as "immigrant Hispanic."

Adriana returned home after her recovery from childbirth; the investigation concluded with the clarification and DNA confirmation that her assailant was her older brother. This brother was sent to Mexico to live with the grandparents, which permitted Adriana's return, and the baby was given up for adoption as planned. The next year, she went to middle school, which was a natural transition to a different, larger group, opening new challenges and possibilities for learning about herself, her thoughts and feelings, her voicing of her own opinions and desires, including her beginning reflections, as she crossed into early teen years, on her and her family's place in their culture. She continued in therapy on her journey of self-discovery, self-awareness, and the articulation of that grounded, authentic voice of her own experience, which is one of the best protections we can build against possible future victimization or abuse. In her own time, in the years ahead, Adriana will continue to make her own meanings of the demands of community and family and the duty she may come to feel she owes to herself to create a life that feels as right and fulfilling as possible to her, hopefully including her own synthesis of all those meanings and their various "pulls."

CONCLUSION

In this series of seven case extracts and discussions—two teenagers, an adult with trauma issues, a couple facing a new stage of life, a young child with multiple problems, an instance of therapist shame in a long-term therapy situation, and finally, a family for which diversity, as it is called in general psychotherapeutic terms, came to the forefront—we hope we have been able to give you a flavor of how Gestalt therapy principles work "on the ground" in a wide range of situations, across a wide diversity of ethnic backgrounds, with wide variation in age, sexual orientation, marital and family status and situation, and socioeconomic and educational class. With one client we shared a great deal of our own "process," and with another little or none. With some we spent more time, as with Carlos, for example, talking about the client's world, while still using our here-and-now contact and relationship in the therapy room as a clarifying reference and a grounding place to return to. Yet, with others we might have done something that looked, from the outside at least, like the reverse of this—spending much more of our time focused on the living experiment of our own relational contact in the present situation while making references to other experiences past and present as clarifying references and comparison points.

We are always focused on our own experience as a source of data and dialogue points and the way the client's experience is organized in the relationship, both inside and in overt behavior and both "here in the room together" and "out there in the world." Our wider point is that Gestalt therapy is never a recipe or a standard set of procedures, nor is the therapist–client relationship just a preliminary stage to "build trust" for the "real therapy" to come. Rather, the therapy is a kind of active dialogic inquiry and exploration with the client into her or his practiced capacities and new experiments in (co-)self-organization of relationship, experience, and meaning. Where are these processes and capacities blocked, stunted, or repetitive in ways that do not serve the client? And where are they well-integrated and free enough from anxiety and dissociation to permit ongoing growth of complexity and deeper meanings and, hopefully, increased participation and satisfaction in living? When we are engaged in this collaborative inquiry (which is, as we have said, Lewin's action research in clinical application), taking apart integrated sequences and styles of contacting in the service of a new integration that serves creativity, connection, and greater depth in living and experiencing, we are practicing Gestalt. This attitude and this practice can then often be integrated usefully with the insights and practices of other methods. We hope that if you, the reader, have a primary identification with another theory family and practice methodology, you may still find many points of intersection and usefulness in the theory story we have told so far and the living cocreative sequences we have shared in the cases here.

5

Evaluation

In this chapter, we take a closer look at the issue of evidence-based out-come research, in terms of the specific research showing Gestalt therapy to be effective and the extensive research base examining the relationship as the healing factor in psychotherapy, a factor which is the fundamental principal of relational Gestalt therapy.

EFFECTIVENESS OF PSYCHOTHERAPY

The good news, both for practitioners and clients of therapy and counseling, is that psychotherapy is generally and broadly effective across an extensive range of populations covering a wide spectrum of problems and diag-nostic categories (for an extensive summative discussion, see Gaudiano & Miller, 2013). An accumulation of large metastudies, some of them covering hundreds—or in a few cases thousands—of other studies, have confirmed

http://dx.doi.org/10.1037/14527-005
Gestalt Therapy, by G. Wheeler and L. Axelsson

that psychotherapy, in contrast to no formal clinical intervention, clearly makes a positive difference in many people's symptoms, suffering, behavior, and lives (American Psychological Association, 2012; Gaudiano & Miller, 2013; Lambert, 2001).

These, among many other studies, show the solid research foundations of psychotherapy, but these general conclusions on the efficacy of psychotherapy raise more specific issues: What is it about psychotherapy specifically that accounts for its effectiveness? What are the positive factors that most influence outcome? Is it theory or a particular methodology (i.e., is one school or approach superior to others or some others)? Or is it something else, some characteristic of the therapist, for instance, that most predicts good outcomes—age or years of experience, say, or particular degrees or something more qualitative in the process?

Large metastudies have examined the factors that most influence the outcomes of therapy. Wampold (2001), for example, reported the following summative findings (which are sustained in numerous other metastudies, such as those cited here as well as in Gaudiano & Miller, 2013):

- Psychotherapy is indeed effective.
- Type of treatment was not found to be a predictive factor.
- Neither the theoretical bases of the techniques used nor the strictness of adherence to those techniques were found to be predictive factors.
- The alliance between the patient and the therapist (e.g., positive and trusting feelings toward the therapist, motivation and collaboration of the client, and empathic response of the therapist) was found to be a key predictive factor.

This does not mean (as Gaudiano & Miller, 2013, emphasized) that no particular methods have been associated with outcome effectiveness. On the contrary, outcome effectiveness has been associated with many different methods, including Gestalt therapy. However, a point that is sometimes overlooked (or perhaps even deliberately obscured, in the interests of promoting or excluding some methods from payment authorization) is that a given method associated with positive outcomes does not in itself demonstrate that (a) it is the method itself that accounts for the effectiveness or (b) that some or many other methods may not be equally effective (conceivably even more so, with certain populations or presenting problems). Indeed, we can say that if it were only method that made the difference, we might expect online or workbook therapy, even without the presence of another person, to show much stronger outcome effectiveness than it does, but this is not the thrust of the research cited earlier, which emphasizes relational factors.

In general, attempts to discriminate relative effectiveness between or among different schools have been much less successful (Luborsky et al., 2002; Miller, Wampold, & Varhely, 2008). None of this detracts from the legitimate interest and duty of providers, payer sources, and policymakers to try to be sure that the interventions they are sponsoring and/or paying for are empirically validated. But it is clear that the methodological challenges in this research area are considerable and that the complexities (and at times, limitations) in examining specific variables, especially theoretical and methodological variables, are huge and often underestimated or completely misunderstood by relevant authorizing agents.

EFFECTIVENESS OF GESTALT THERAPY

Where does this leave the evidence-based outcome status of Gestalt therapy, one of those many methods for which outcome research is sparse? The challenges of determining adherence to a core Gestalt practice methodology are especially daunting for a method that explicitly prizes creativity and experiment and explicitly makes use of the authentic, present (and thus variable) "felt" relational experience between therapist and client in the therapy session. In this book we have emphasized that Gestalt is not a fixed method in any protocol or step-by-step sense; rather, it is a set of principles and understandings about how human experience becomes coherent and works, how we orient relationally in a cosubjective field, and how we experiment, learn, and above all, create as a unique species and in our own unique experiences, relationships, and lives. Given these principles, goals, and values, how can we assess which therapists or which behaviors are or are not "Gestalt-adherent" so as to compare outcomes by method or other variable (Stevens, Stringfellow, Wakelin, & Waring, 2011; Strümpfel, 2006)?

We propose a two-part answer to this question. First, we note the outcome research, cited earlier, that surveyed a range of methods including those labeled as *person-centered, interpersonal, relational,* or *present- or problem-centered* and that was broadly and meaningfully coextensive with a Gestalt approach. These studies and metastudies show clear positive benefit for these interpersonal approaches to a degree comparable with the more researched behaviorally focused methods. More work is needed to demonstrate that all the terms are validly coextensive with each other and with relational Gestalt therapy, but we believe this could be done and would result in meaningful groupings of results for the "relational and experiential" therapies.

Research on the efficacy of Gestalt therapy has shown that it is equal, and in some aspects superior, to other therapy methods such as cognitive behavior therapy (CBT). Strümpfel (2006) completed a meta-analysis comparing Gestalt therapy (as a stand-alone method and in combination with focused-expressive psychotherapy and process oriented psychotherapy) with CBT. The results showed no statistically significant difference between the methods when looking at the overall level of treatment. When investigating some of the subcategories that were part of the studies, one significant difference was found: Patients treated with Gestalt therapy were found to have a greater improvement in interpersonal problem-solving skills.

Azar and Asadnia (2013) conducted a study with female college students with poor sleep quality, comparing treatment with CBT and with Gestalt group therapy. Students receiving treatment showed significant improvement in their sleep quality compared with the control group, but there was not a significant difference between the group that received CBT and the group that received Gestalt group therapy.

A research project completed in the United Kingdom used the clinical outcomes in routine evaluation (CORE) system. This system is the most widely used approach for auditing, evaluating, and measuring outcomes for psychotherapy and counseling services in the United Kingdom, with about 50,000 client results saved in the CORE National Research Database. A total of 135 clients treated by Gestalt therapists participated in the study. When comparing the results from these clients using the CORE method to assess effectiveness of treatment, Gestalt therapy appeared to be as effective as other modalities (Stevens et al., 2011).

The work cited earlier showed that the strongest factor cluster in predicting positive therapeutic outcome is not level or years of experience or choice of method (or adherence to that method), but a recurrent cluster of factors relating to the qualities of the relationship in the therapist–client contact and process. These factors include alliance, empathy, goal consensus and collaboration, congruence and genuineness, active openness to client feedback, repair of ruptures, and the like (Norcross, 2011; Stiles, Barkham, Mellor-Clark, & Connell, 2008; see also Wampold, 2001). These findings do not mean that training, theoretical knowledge, professional experience, diagnostic capacity, and other such factors are not important; rather, they cannot substitute for the more overriding relational factor: the capacity to enter into and conduct a relationship with another person in a way that makes him or her feel seen, understood, supported in her or his goals, and generally less alone with the problems and situations that have been distressing or hindering her or him in the universal quest that all of us share, dealing with the challenges short and long term that come up in the course of living, and where possible, moving beyond just coping to achieve a sense of connectedness, satisfaction, and meaning in life.

Take, for instance, the quality of *alliance*, which has been described and measured and which was identified as one of the strongest predictors of treatment success (e.g., Wampold, 2001). Bordin (1994) suggested that alliance in the early stages of treatment is built principally on a positive emotional bond between therapist and client (e.g., trust, respect, liking), their ability to agree on the goals of the treatment, and their establishment of a mutual consensus on the tasks that form the substance of the specific therapy (e.g., homework, Socratic dialogue, free association). Alliance may then be rated from three separate perspectives: client, therapist, and observer, with client and observer ratings being both quite similar and also better predictors of outcome than the therapist's evaluation. Although the difference among the perspectives in the meta-analysis of Norcross (2011) was not found to be statistically significant, the cautionary message to therapists is clear: We may be naturally biased in our evaluation of our therapeutic effectiveness.

Likewise, the quality of *empathy* can be described more behaviorally and has been shown repeatedly to be another of the key predictors of therapy effectiveness. Empathy is the capacity to "enter into" or attune to the feelings the client is experiencing and to communicate that attunement to the client. In this volume we have discussed this quality in several instances as the capacity to "show up" in a personal and genuine way, as, for example, when we allow ourselves to register in our body and emotions the states the client is experiencing and reporting (or at times, experiencing but not reporting, which can become the basis for sensitive inquiry in Gestalt therapy, as, for example, by saying, "I feel a sinking feeling in my stomach as you talk about this—or a tightness in my throat, a burning in my eyes, etc.—is that how you feel it too?"). Communicating this to the client is also key: It is the client's perception of how empathic the therapist is that predicts outcome better than either the therapist's or an observer's perception of therapist empathy (Bohart, 2002).

This leads us to a third qualitative relational descriptor, one that is perhaps less intuitively understood than alliance and empathy: *congruence*. By congruence we mean that the therapist's interventions and responses are both consonant with those of the client (i.e., empathic, in the sense described earlier) and self-congruent; they convey a sense of the therapist as an integrated person with embodied states and named emotional expressions that are consonant with her or his other verbal expressions ("The words and the music match up," as one of our clients put it) and with other manifestations of personality, such as opinions, style, and even dress and setting decor (to the extent that the therapist may have been able to personalize it, depending on the setting). As clients, we "spin stories" about our therapists, based at times on the most minimal signs and clues (indeed, in Gestalt, we would insist that this kind of "projective" activity is inherent and necessary to our social orientation as human beings). This research has shown that trust in therapy is fostered—as in other kinds of relationships—when the sources of information and speculation about the other person produce a coherent picture we can count on and relax into (so that even surprises, when they come, stand out against a more stable ground and enrich rather than undermine the relationship). Here, too, Norcross (2011), along with many others, identified congruence in this sense as one of the strongly significant predictors of effectiveness in therapy.

This brings us to the second part of our answer to the question of the effectiveness of Gestalt therapy. In Gestalt therapy, relationship building is not just preliminary to therapy or an early stage of therapy; it is the heart of the therapy, and one might rightly say that in Gestalt, relationship building and the exploration of all the issues it involves constitutes the therapy. In other words, these qualitative relational dimensions of the therapeutic process, which have emerged again and again over the past 4 decades of empirical outcomes research in psychotherapy as strong—perhaps the strongest factors in therapeutic effectiveness (e.g., Smith & Glass, 1977; Stiles et al., 2008; as well as more contemporary research: Stevens et al., 2011)—are actually the meat of Gestalt theory and method and the heart of Gestalt therapist training.

6

Future Developments

Every living thing depends on the twin dynamic principles of conservation and change. Together, these two poles define life: Without change,
an organism has no new input and nourishment and soon withers and
dies. Without conservation, the organism has no flexible boundary and no
criteria of selection and soon disperses into the wider environment. These
are basic Gestalt psychology principles, and they are inherent to any process of life, including change, growth, contact, and the in-and-out flow of
mutual nourishment that distinguishes us and also embeds us in a wider
shared field. Restoring the balance between the old and the new, stability
and new learning, established "ground" and new "figure" is the *restoration
of growth*, which is the central aim of Gestalt therapy.

These same living principles apply to theories and methodologies as
well. Without the capacity to take in and digest new needs and conditions
in our ever-changing field, a theory becomes a fossil, just a cookbook on

http://dx.doi.org/10.1037/14527-006
Gestalt Therapy, by G. Wheeler and L. Axelsson

the shelf, with little application to the here-and-now world. Without a strong basis in core principles, a theory does not offer any foundation for further growth. In this volume we have offered you an account of Gestalt therapy that is not a cookbook but that rests on a vital foundation of core principles that can continue to generate and accommodate new growth in the fertile creative tradition of Lewin, Goodman, the Perlses, and generations of Gestalt teachers and writers since that time, a number of whom we cited throughout Chapter 3.

What lies ahead? We believe that in the coming years Gestalt theory and method will continue to evolve in three lively, burgeoning areas: (a) neuroscience and the ongoing research revolution in interpersonal neurobiology (Siegel, 2012), further expanding and refining our understanding of the healing effects of relational therapy and how to support and enhance those effects; (b) the treatment of trauma informed by this revolution and the growing knowledge base offered to Gestalt and other methods on nervous system activation, on relational processes and effects at a nervous system level, and on healing from trauma; and (c) the application of these ideas and practices, based on a relational field model, to community, educational, and lifelong development issues and especially to the ever-growing needs in the areas of child development, early childhood intervention, and parent education and support areas and issues, taking our therapy practices beyond the therapy room and into our shared world of public programs and policy. Next, we briefly take a deeper look at each of these areas in turn.

THE NEUROSCIENTIFIC REVOLUTION

Recently researchers have begun to understand some of the ways in which our cognitive and emotional experiences and patterns have a neurobiological substrate. That substrate, we know now, is mostly not fixed at birth but becomes shaped and patterned through the relationships we have all through life, especially during our first years of development (Panksepp, 2009). We can now see the dichotomy of "nature versus nurture" as a false one. For human beings, as evolutionary biologist Paul Ehrlich (2000) put it, nature *is* nurture.

Not only is the long-standing core principle of Gestalt—that life is about taking up relationships, and therapy has to do with restoring balance and flow in that natural contact process—being validated almost daily by new research in neuroscience and interpersonal neurobiology (Siegel, 2012), but we are also learning more all the time about how that happens, in ever-greater detail. Thus, not only are we strengthened and heartened (and joined more and more) as relational Gestalt therapists in our insistence on the key function of the therapist–client relationship in healing, but we are also guided in our practices to become ever-more skilled in supporting a greater healing presence and impact. Today more than ever it is important for therapists to stay abreast of these new findings as they apply to our field, as part of our own quest to learn how to better use therapeutic attunement and the coconstruction (with the client) of those facilitative environments for lasting growth in our clients' relationships and lives.

Another aspect in which neuroscience supports relational Gestalt therapy is the strong emphasis on the therapist's presence in the room, as a relational environment of meeting, holding, and regulating, an area we will see develop even further in the future to provide better treatment. At the edge of this learning, for many therapists, is attending to our own arousal state as part of that relational environment. This means body awareness as well as a clear knowledge of and sensitivity to our own issues and triggers for reactivity. Our Gestalt tradition of moving beyond just "story content" to felt, embodied, and relational experience in the present moment means that we are well-positioned to adopt the applications of this research explosion and integrate them into our living practices and relationships in the therapeutic setting.

Given this, it is disturbing to note that the current trend in training programs for therapists is to have minimal or no requirements for trainees to engage deeply in the therapeutic process as clients. In our view, a relationship with a mentor therapist, who may evolve into a mentor consultant over time, is one of the most essential training prerequisites for psychotherapists. We believe this is true for any theory and method and for Gestalt work in particular, based as it is on creativity, individual difference and deep belonging, the power of embodied affect, and the goal of increased capacity for ever-more complex wholes of meaning and relationship. To imagine embarking on that complex work without a deep voyage through one's own history and capacities for contact, complexity, and creativity makes no sense and may in fact be a path toward rigidity or damage to the self and others. Key is the relational stance. Because we build relationship by inquiring deeply into the phenomenology of our client's world (and thereby learning more about our own), we need a strong base of contact capacity ourselves to act as the "holding relationship" for our client's development.

A fuller Gestalt articulation of developmental theory, drawing on neuroscience to emphasize the way earlier patterning becomes encoded and then governs later development, supports our differential focus on particular areas of a person's life that are moving and changing, in contrast to those that are stuck in old pattern reactions. Such a theory development helps us to understand the developmental history of each capacity in turn, in terms of the kinds of support that were present when that particular area was first becoming stuck or (to use a common developmental image) arrested. This kind of view also helps therapists see what supports are needed for the client to be able to relax the too-rigid reactive pattern of those challenges and resume a path of growth and change in that area.

Neuroscience has already taught us that our brains develop physically through relational process and that these relationally based patterns will set a "template" for how we continue to select, integrate, and use new experience and learning throughout life. It is not just a matter of cognitive processing: Extensive neuroscientific research around regulation has shown how the structure and regulation of our nervous system develop and are affected to a large degree by relationships in our lives. As J. R. Schore and Schore (2008) pointed out, contemporary attachment theory has now become, through research, a regulation theory.

TRAUMA TREATMENT

Research in neuroscience also influences our work involving strong emotional activation, the treatment of trauma, and the regulation of the nervous system (and coregulation, in the course of relational therapy). Today in psychotherapy we have moved beyond the time when explosive emotional discharge for its own sake was accepted uncritically as a positive and healing event. This does not mean that expressing strong emotions does not have a crucial place in therapy; we believe it does. But that expression should be contextualized by a deeper understanding on the therapist's part of the dynamics of the brain and nervous system. The question is one of balance and support; it is the therapist's role to support the client in experimenting safely to find the right balance at any specific moment between strong expression and well-integrated containment (with therapist support, especially in the early stages of trying out a "deeper dive" into unfamiliar emotional expression).

Siegel (2012) wrote, "One's thinking or behavior can become disrupted if arousal moves beyond the boundaries of the window of tolerance" (p. 254). From a relational Gestalt point of view, a person who breaks through his or her window of tolerance will have a limited ability to make any kind of flexible contact with his or her environment. More likely, the client will have to revert to a "fallback" contact pattern, something older and more rigid that manages the too-stressful arousal—likely the kind of learned dysfunction that has caused problems in her or his life and was a reason bringing him or her to therapy. The risk is also that the pattern of feeling out of control and helpless will once more be reinforced by hyperarousal. This does not mean we have to avoid strong feelings in therapy (or in life); rather, we must work with the client collaboratively, in constant communication, to try to stay within that "therapeutic window," the client's optimal learning zone of the moment, the zone of arousal in which the client can experience and still manage and process highly charged emotional and traumatic material (Resneck-Sannes, 2011).

This also means making sure that these expressions of strong emotion are followed by completion, recovery (a quieting of the arousal state), and integration. The new learning takes place in the integration stage, in which a broader background of experience and emotions becomes attached to and integrated with this more disruptive experience and the client can find and make new meanings about events, feelings, relationships, and possibilities in his or her life. As Klopstech (2005) pointed out, a cathartic experience is not in itself healing but may have the potential to be healing if it is followed by an integration into the self, significant relationships, and everyday life. As further research in the neuroscience of learning reveals more about how new learning happens, we believe relational Gestalt therapy is well-positioned to continue to profit from this new knowledge.

A direct outgrowth of this new research in neuroscience is a transformation in our understanding and treatment of recovery and healing from trauma (experiences, at times assaultive, which have overwhelmed and to some extent disabled the full integration of our capacities at a nervous system level). More recently this understanding has included the key idea of *developmental trauma* (van der Kolk, 2005), which extends the idea of lasting traumatic effects to include experiences that may not be specific or violent assaults but that can be a larger childhood history and pattern of abuse, traumatic events, and/or neglect.

We have seen, especially in Chapter 4, that these developments in neuroscience have already started to inform our work with clients who are dealing with symptoms of trauma, as, for example, in the case of Diana. With clients who have a trauma history (early or recent abuse trauma or developmental trauma), the issue of regulation of the nervous system becomes even more important. In Diana's case, for example, this meant offering attuned relational support for her to regulate and relax her panic or "freeze" response enough to discover and develop her more empowering "fight" response after years in which freeze was the only reaction her nervous system could support and access.

BEYOND THE THERAPY SESSION

As we have emphasized all through this volume, in the relational field Gestalt model we can never fully, usefully view the person, the emotion, or the behavior outside a larger relational and whole-field context. In the Gestalt perspective, we are all part of a unified web of relationships: What affects the field in one place affects it (and us) in other places and ways as well.

Thus, as we see in the cases of Carlos, Daisy, and Adriana, we often have to think and practice outside the box of the therapy room, drawing on the settings and resources of the greater community. Especially when working with children and teenagers, who developmentally are more embedded in their immediate field, our ability to influence the people surrounding the client is key to promoting greater change. Thus, for example, in Gestalt work with children and adolescents especially, we may find ourselves talking with teachers and other providers, designing in-class or at-home strategies, giving homework to individuals and couples, and in general taking a "field view" of the client's life—potentially at every age. As the stigma against therapy lessens in our society, it becomes easier to extend the therapy outside the therapy room, and with our strong grounding in field theory and the notion that to promote change we have to modify supports in a person's field, going out into the community to support the client is one of the natural next steps we foresee in the development of relational Gestalt therapy.

In this way we can see where some of the older, more rigid boundaries between therapy and counseling and coaching, community and organizational work, and advocacy are loosening in ways we see as generally positive. As we expand on these modalities of supporting our clients, we open up to different interventions, all of which support each individual client in her or his field to promote the change he or she is seeking in therapy and in life.

As Lewin (1951) reminded us, by the terms of the basic Gestalt psychology model of awareness and perception, we can never actually take in everything; we naturally have to make boundaries of relevancy to frame any situation and attempt to understand it and intervene. Field-relational theory helps us to remember that the larger field is always there, always conditioning and constraining options in thinking and behaving, often in ways that we are not immediately aware of. Thus, as relational Gestalt therapists (and others), we all benefit from the reminder to step back, look at the client and her or his situation more widely, and take in underlying present factors that are affecting the client's life and our relational process in therapy. My health and best functioning, like that of my clients, can never be completely separated from the supportive or unsupportive conditions of the wider field—socioeconomic, cultural, environmental, and relational at many levels. Thus, therapists are called on more today than ever before to be advocates, public spokespeople, and activists in the ways that are most natural and available to us—in speaking and writing, in our communities, and in public policy debates on the allocation of support and resources in society.

An outstanding example of a new and innovative approach to the integration of psychotherapy, public health, and community activism is the work of The Relational Center (TRC) in Los Angeles (http://www.relationalcenter.org). On the basis of the Gestalt relational model in combination with public narrative work, TRC uses a pioneering training and empowerment approach to bring low-fee and no-fee mental health and community-building services to an underserved and marginalized urban population. In addition, they also train professionals to apply the model in other venues in several countries (see Fairfield, 2013; Ganz, 2009).

7

Summary

All through these chapters we have presented a Gestalt model that is not a recipe or a set of techniques but a fundamental methodology for working with people in psychotherapy and (with appropriate modifications) in a wide range of other settings and modalities as well. The model is based on relationship, creative growth, embodied emotional experience, and a new understanding of support, and it is grounded in the rich century-long tradition of Gestalt psychological research. That underlying research tradition established a set of fundamental assumptions about our cognitive and emotional process that, as we have argued here, have long since become foundational in the basic organizing paradigm for understanding human process in contemporary psychology across many different fields. From those principles comes our understanding of the selective and constructive process model of perception, cognition, and learning, principles that at the broadest level underlie today's emergent

http://dx.doi.org/10.1037/14527-007
Gestalt Therapy, by G. Wheeler and L. Axelsson

fields of cognitive neuroscience and interpersonal neurobiology. These burgeoning new fields, in turn, are now setting the agenda for the ongoing evolution of our wider field and our relational Gestalt model.

As we established in Chapters 2 and 3, an additional foundational principle of Gestalt psychology is field theory: All our perceptions (and we ourselves) are in and of the field, both our inner and outer field of experience. We are not external observers of our experiential field; rather, we are coparticipants in that field, making subjective interpretations and meanings. This also means, as we have pointed out, that we view the dichotomy between inner and outer as an oversimplification because we know today that what is viewed as the inner world (of thoughts, feelings, values and beliefs) is both a subjective construction and a reflection of our past and present relational experiences, whereas our outer field is not an objective picture of "what's there" but an interpretation conditioned by prior assumptions and selective biases that color and constrain our perceptions. Thus, both the concepts of inner and outer worlds of experience have to be relativized; the two realms of subjective experience interpenetrate and codetermine each other more than we generally realize, and our behavior emerges out of a whole interpreted field of perception.

If our actions and ways of relating and contacting our environment are too heavily conditioned by past relationships and learning, not taking enough account of what is new and different in our current situation (and in our current available supports and resources), we view the world and organize our behavior from what we have been calling all through these chapters a *fixed Gestalt*. Most often it is this repetitive, unfulfilling process that leads the client to seek out therapy. The therapeutic relationship makes the "safe emergency" of therapy safe enough to relax some of these reactive patterns so that the client can begin to experience and experiment with new feelings, new behaviors, and new ways of living and relating to the world.

Throughout this volume—and especially in Chapter 4—our intention has been to give you, the reader, a sense of how relational Gestalt therapy unfolds and can lead to experiment and lasting change in the therapy room and beyond. The use of a present-centered model that regards the here-and-now relationship in the room as authentic and real, we believe, best serves the transfer of those new experiences in therapy to the ongoing challenges of the rest of life.

As we have discussed, a strong common thread in all the case narratives in Chapter 4, and one of the hallmarks of relational Gestalt therapy, is the therapist's use of self. The therapist is not a detached observer but a fully engaged participant and observer—while we set aside our own issues and agenda in the service of the client, we share selectively from our own present experience in the session, recognizing that whatever happens in any relationship has elements of cocreation, in which both participants contribute and assent to (or in dire cases may have been coerced or have submitted to) what happens between them. As therapists (and simply as people), we know how difficult it can be for our clients (or for us ourselves) to see their and our role in creating or at least inviting the painful difficulties we may get into, recurrently and often mystifyingly, in particular kinds of situations and relationships or in life in general. By understanding the present relational process in this way, we open up a whole additional dimension of useful "real-time" data for the client—namely, information about how the client is affecting the field of supported relational possibilities—which is always, in this model, a cocreation of both parties.

An additional linking theme that cuts across the chapters and the case narratives is relational Gestalt therapy's focus on the key Gestalt concept of *support*. Support is all those conditions (inner and outer, as we have sharply relativized those terms) that facilitate a given experience or behavior and/or inhibit other possible experiences and behaviors in a situation. In the process we have called into question our strongly individualistic Western culture, where drawing support from "outside the self" can be viewed as problematic dependency, even weakness and danger. In contrast, contemporary Gestalt therapy rests on a radically transformed understanding of the dynamics of support and a new articulation of a Gestalt theory of change based on these relational field dynamics.

Because the message of this Gestalt change theory, we believe, is one of the most important takeaways of this book (and of the Gestalt model for practitioners of every methodology today), we repeat it here: Behavior and experience are integrated constructions in an organized, subjective context of perceived and felt supports (and inhibitions, which we can view as constraints or negative supports). This articulation of change theory emerges out of the "mapping" Lewin (1936, 1951) was talking about, as a metaphor for our integrated process: What is my situation (as I perceive it)? Where am I trying to go? What am I trying to cope with or avoid? In relation to that, what and where are my supports for going toward my intention (or avoiding a fear)? On the basis of this map, Gestalt change theory tells us that for any change to be effective and sustainable, there must be a corresponding change in the underlying field conditions of support. Whatever my experience and my behavior, it will be based on this subjective map, a map of supports (including the negative or aversive features of that field; a negative support for a particular experience or course of action is at the same time a support for going a different way). Stated like this, the theory of change sounds self-evident, like any true observation about our behavior and process, but we believe that if you keep this in mind in the therapy hour, you will find the difference it can make to be profound.

Given these nonrigid and flexible ways of working in relational Gestalt therapy, research based on this theory can become a challenge, but as we pointed out in Chapter 5, the branch of research we suggest is the one focusing more on the processes of therapy: the relational factors. The research done on these relational factors (alliance, empathy, goal consensus and collaboration, congruence and genuineness, active openness to client feedback, repair of ruptures, and the like) shows that they are the measurable empirical variables that affect the outcome of therapy the most.

With that as a base, we hope that by this point you have a good feel, as well as a theoretical understanding, of how relational Gestalt therapy is used and practiced today. Because this is a discussion about Gestalt, we add explicitly here that the articulation of theory and methodology we have given you (although widely shared among leading teachers, writers, and practitioners of our generations of Gestalt therapy and related applications today around the world) is still just that: an articulation of our interpretive understandings, informed now by a combined half century between us of interactive dialogue with our colleagues, students, and especially our clients, both in Gestalt and widely in enriching conversation with advocates of many other methods and views. Although still agreeing on a common set of theoretical assumptions and attitudes as a shared base, others might articulate these points differently, with the unique creative foci and emphases from their life and professional experiences, needs, and primary concerns. That kind of creative difference is taken as a healthy given in Gestalt theory and work.

We are all eclectic therapists today, in that we draw from the rich cornucopia of methods and techniques for dealing with diverse particular populations, particularly challenging problems, and widely varying practice settings that characterize our world. As we do this, we try (sometimes awkwardly) to relate those gifts and insights to our "home" theories and methodologies—those particular theoretical perspectives whose assumptions and values stand up best to our reflection and scrutiny and that feel most deeply congruent with our own basic beliefs and values about human nature, human relationships, and human process. Because Gestalt therapy rests on Gestalt psychology, a system that was built on inquiry about human process at the most basic level (before being applied to therapeutic and systemic issues and problems), we find it particularly useful in sorting through this eclectic therapy landscape in today's diverse, complex, multi-problem world. In this way our necessary eclecticism becomes an informed choicefulness, as we contextualize the different techniques and approaches on offer with regard to how they serve and support attuned relationship, full presence and contact, free experiment, and support in relation to particular clients at particular times.

Over the past half century, Gestalt therapy has had a deep and pervasive influence on most other major schools of psychotherapy, spurring more present focus, more authenticity and contact in the client–therapist relationship, greater attention to support, and more focus on challenge, growth, client strengths, and what today is often termed *positive psychology*. This influence has not been one-way; over these same years, Gestalt has gained greatly from the psychodynamic and cognitive behavior schools in the areas of attachment theory, developmental theory, narrative theory, attention to unexamined beliefs and their constrictive role in behavior and experience, and the study of creativity. This rapprochement does not mean that meaningful differences between and among the major schools of psychotherapy do not still exist or are unimportant. Rather, each orientation represents a unique center of understanding or point of view on human nature and human process. Whatever school or method you identify most closely with, now or in the future, we hope that through this volume you have gained an insight into the many riches of relational Gestalt, together with particular insights and practices you can apply to any method or mode you find yourself working in.

Once again, we wish you courage and heart for the work you are doing, now and in the future, and blessings for your journey.

Suggested Readings

Clemmens, M. C. (2005). *Getting beyond sobriety: Clinical approaches to long-term recovery.* Hillsdale, NJ: Analytic Press.

Frank, R. (2001). *Body of awareness: A somatic and developmental approach to psychotherapy.* Hillsdale, NJ: Analytic Press.

Frank, R., & La Barre, F. (2010). *The first year and the rest of your life: Movement, development and psychotherapeutic change.* New York, NY: Routledge, Taylor & Francis.

Hycner, R., & Jacobs, L. (1996). *The healing relationship in Gestalt therapy: A dialogic-self psychological approach.* Highland, NY: Gestalt Journal Press.

Jacobs, L., & Hycner, R. (Eds.). (2009). *Relational approaches in gestalt therapy.* New York, NY: Routledge, Taylor & Francis.

Kepner, J. I. (1987). *Body process: A Gestalt approach to working with the body in psychotherapy.* New York, NY: Gardner Press.

Kepner, J. I. (1996). *Healing tasks: Psychotherapy with adult survivors of sexual abuse.* San Francisco, CA: Jossey-Bass.

Lee, R. G. (2008). *The secret language of intimacy: Releasing the hidden power in couple relationships.* New York, NY: Routledge, Taylor & Francis.

Lee, R. G., & Harris, N. (2011). *Relational child, relational brain: Development and therapy in childhood and adolescence.* New York, NY: Routledge, Taylor & Francis.

Lee, R. G., & Wheeler, G. (1996). *The voice of shame: Silence and connection in psychotherapy.* San Francisco, CA: Jossey-Bass.

Levine Bar-Yoseph, T. (Ed.) (2005). *The bridge: Dialogues across cultures.* Metairie, LA: Gestalt Institute of New Orleans Press.

McConville, M. (1995). *Adolescence: Psychotherapy and the emergent self.* San Francisco, CA: Jossey-Bass.

McConville, M., & Wheeler, G. (Eds.). (2001). *The heart of development: Gestalt approaches to working with children, adolescents and their worlds: Vol. II. Adolescence.* Hillsdale, NJ: Analytic Press.

Melnick, J., & Nevis, E. (2013). *Mending the world: Social healing interventions by gestalt practitioners worldwide.* New York, NY: Routledge Taylor & Francis.

Mortola, P. (2006). *Windowframes: Learning the art of gestalt play therapy the Oaklander way.* New York, NY: Routledge Taylor & Francis.

Nevis, E. (Ed.). (1987). *Organizational consulting: A gestalt approach.* New York, NY: Routledge Taylor & Francis.

Nevis, E. (Ed.). (1993). *Gestalt therapy perspectives and applications.* New York, NY: Gardner Press.

Oaklander, V. (1988). *Windows to our children: A gestalt approach to children and adolescents.* Highland, NY: Gestalt Journal Press.

Oaklander, V. (2007). *Hidden treasure: A map to the child's inner self.* London, England: Karnac Books.

Perls, F. S., Hefferline, R., & Goodman, P. (1994). *Gestalt therapy: Excitement and growth in the human personality.* New York, NY: Gestalt Journal Press. (Original work published 1951)

Polster, E., & Polster, M. (1974). *Gestalt therapy integrated: Contours of theory and practice.* New York, NY: Vintage.

Polster, E., & Polster, M. (1999). *From the radical center: The heart of gestalt therapy.* Cleveland, OH: Gestalt Institute of Cleveland Press.

Stoehr, T. (Ed.). (1994). *Crazy hope and finite experience: Final essays of Paul Goodman.* San Francisco, CA: Jossey-Bass.

Stoehr, T. (1994). *Here, now, next: Paul Goodman and the origins of gestalt therapy.* Hillsdale, NJ: Analytic Press.

Ullman, D., & Wheeler, G. (2009). *Cocreating the field: Intention and practice in the age of complexity.* New York, NY: Routledge Taylor & Francis.

Wheeler, G. (1991). *Gestalt reconsidered: A new approach to contact and resistance.* New York, NY: Gardner Press.

Wheeler, G. (2000). *Beyond individualism: Toward a new understanding of self, relation, and experience.* Hillsdale, NJ: Analytic Press.

Wheeler, G. (2002). The developing field: Toward a Gestalt developmental model. In G. Wheeler & M. McConville (Eds.), *The heart of development: Gestalt approaches to working with children, adolescents, and their worlds: Vol. 1. Childhood* (pp. 37–84). Hillsdale, NJ: Analytic Press/GestaltPress.

Wheeler, G. (2005). Culture self and field: A gestalt guide to the age of complexity. In T. Levine (Ed.), *The bridge: Dialogues across cultures* (pp. 43–68). Metairie, LA: Gestalt Institute Press.

Wheeler, G., & McConville, M. (Eds.). (2002). *The heart of development: Gestalt approaches to working with children, adolescents and their worlds: Vol. 1. Childhood.* Hillsdale NY: Analytic Press.

Yontef, G. M. (1993). *Awareness, dialogue and process.* Highland, NY: Gestalt Journal Press.

Zinker, J. (1977). *Creative process in gestalt therapy.* New York, NY: Random House.

References

Allport, G. (1954). *The nature of prejudice.* Reading, MA: Addison-Wesley.

American Psychological Association. (Producer). (2012). *Three approaches to psychotherapy with a female client* [DVD]. Available from http://www.apa.org/pubs/videos/4310889.aspx

Axelsson, L. (in press). Gestalt-based trauma recovery with couples. In M. Kraus, A. Roberts, & G. Wheeler (Eds.), *The couple in the field: Gestalt relational field therapy with couples.* New York, NY: Routledge Taylor & Francis.

Azar, F. S., & Asadnia, S. (2013). Efficacy of cognitive behavior therapy and gestalt therapy on poor sleep quality among college female students with headache. *Journal of Education, Psychology and Social Sciences, 1,* 15–24.

Bateson, G. (1979, September). *It takes two to know one.* Paper presented at the meeting of the Esalen Summer Teacher Talk Series, Big Sur, CA.

Beisser, A. (1970). The paradoxical theory of change. In J. Fagan & I. Shepard (Eds.), *Gestalt therapy now: Theory, techniques, application* (pp. 77–80). Palo Alto, CA: Science and Behavior Books.

Bloom, D. (2009). A quest for gestalt therapy group process: Group process as self process. *Studies in Gestalt/Dialogical Bridges, 3,* 25–38.

Bohart, A. E. (2002). Empathy. In J. C. Norcross (Ed.), *Psychotherapy relationships that work* (pp. 89–108). New York, NY: Oxford University Press.

Bordin, E. S. (1994). Theory and research on the working alliance: New directions. In A. O. Horvath & L. S. Greenberg (Eds.), *The working alliance: Theory, research, and practice* (pp. 13–37). New York, NY: Wiley.

Boring, E. (1950). *A history of experimental psychology.* New York, NY: Appleton-Century-Crofts.

Bowlby, J. (1994). *En trygg bas—Kliniska tillämpningar av bindningsteorin* [A secure base—Clinical applications of bonding theory]. Stockholm, Sweden: Bokförlaget Natur och Kultur.

Brentano, F. (1988). *Philosophical investigations on space, time, and the continuum.* London, England: Croom Helm.

Clemmens, M. C. (2005). *Getting beyond sobriety: Clinical approaches to long-term recovery.* Hillsdale, NJ: Analytic Press.

Cozolino, L. (2010). *The neuroscience of psychotherapy: Healing the social brain.* New York, NY: Norton.

Ehrenfels, C. (1890). Ueber gestaltqualitäten [On gestalt properties]. *Vierteljahrsschrift für wissenschaftliche Philosophie, 14,* 242–292.

Ehrlich, P. (2000). *Human natures: Genes, cultures, and the human prospect.* Washington, DC: Island Press.

Ellis, W. (Ed.). (1938). *A source book of Gestalt psychology.* London, England: Routledge Kegan Paul. doi:10.1037/11496-000

Fairfield, M. (2013). The relational movement. *British Gestalt Journal, 22,* 22–35.

Feder, B., & Ronall, R. (Eds.). (1980). *Beyond the hot seat.* New York, NY: Brunner/ Mazel.

Frank, R. (2001). *Body of awareness: A somatic and developmental approach to psychotherapy.* Cambridge, MA: GestaltPress.

Freud, A. (1937). *The ego and the mechanisms of defense.* London, England: Hogarth Press.

Freud, S. (1965). *New introductory lectures on psychoanalysis.* New York, NY: Norton. (Original work published 1933)

Freud, S. (2005). *On murder, mourning and melancholia.* London, England: Penguin.

Ganz, M. (2009). *Why David sometimes wins: Strategy, leadership and the California agricultural movement.* New York, NY: Oxford University Press.

Gaudiano, B. A., & Miller, I. W. (2013). The evidence-based practice of psychotherapy: Facing the challenges that lie ahead. *Clinical Psychology Review, 33,* 813–824. doi:10.1016/j.cpr.2013.04.004

Gergen, K. J. (2011). *Relational being: Beyond self and community.* New York, NY: Oxford University Press.

Gibson, J. (1950). *The perception of the visual world.* Boston, MA: Houghton Mifflin.

Goldstein, K. (1939). *The organism.* Boston, MA: American Book Company.

Goldstein, K. (1940). *Human nature in the light of psychopathology.* Cambridge, MA: Harvard University Press. doi:10.4159/harvard.9780674492103

Goodman, P. (1951). Novelty, excitement and growth (Vol. 2). In F. H. Perls, R. Hefferline, & P. Goodman, *Gestalt therapy: Excitement and growth in the human personality.* New York, NY: Julian Press.

Goodman, P. (1962). *Compulsory miseducation.* New York, NY: Horizon.

Henle, M. (1961). *Documents of Gestalt psychology.* Berkeley, CA: University of California Press.

Hrdy, S. B. (2009). *Mothers and others: The evolutionary origins of mutual understanding.* Cambridge, MA: Oxford University Press.

Husserl, E. (1990). *On the phenomenology of the consciousness of internal time.* Dordrecht, Netherlands: Kluwer. (Original work published 1928)

Jacobs, L., & Hycner, R. (Eds.). (2009). *Relational approaches in gestalt therapy.* New York, NY: Routledge, Taylor & Francis.

James, W. (2007). *Principles of psychology.* New York, NY: Cosimo. (Original work published 1890)

Kant, I. (1983). *The critique of pure reason.* North Clarendon, VT: Tuttle. (Original work published 1781)

Kepner, J. I. (1987). *Body process: A gestalt approach to working with the body in psychotherapy.* New York, NY: Gardner Press.

Kepner, J. I. (1996). *Healing tasks: Psychotherapy with adult survivors of sexual abuse.* San Francisco, CA: Jossey-Bass.

Klopstech, A. (2005). Catharsis and self-regulation revisited: Scientific and clinical considerations. *Bioenergetic Analysis, 15,* 101–133.

Koehler, K. (1947). *Gestalt psychology.* New York, NY: Liveright.

Koffka, K. (1924). Introduction. In W. Ellis (Ed.), *A source book in Gestalt psychology* (pp. xii–xiv). London, England: Routledge & Kegan Paul.

Koffka, K. (1935). *Principles of Gestalt psychology.* New York, NY: Harcourt, Brace & World.

Köhler, W. (1938a). Physical gestalten. In W. Ellis (Ed.), *A source book in Gestalt psychology* (pp. 17–54). London, England: Routledge & Kegan Paul. doi:10.1037/11496-003

Köhler, W. (1938b). Simple structural functions in the chimpanzee and in the chicken. In W. Ellis (Ed.), *A source book in Gestalt psychology* (pp. 217–227). London, England: Routledge & Kegan Paul. doi:10.1037/11496-018

Korzybski, A. (1994). *Science and sanity.* New York, NY: Institute for General Semantics.

Lambert, M. (2001). Research summary on the therapeutic relationship and psychotherapy outcome. *Psychotherapy: Theory, Research, Practice, Training, 38,* 357–361. doi:10.1037/0033-3204.38.4.357

Lee, R. (1996). Shame and the gestalt model. In R. Lee & G. Wheeler (Eds.), *The voice of shame: Silence and connection in psychotherapy* (pp. 3–21). San Francisco, CA: Jossey-Bass.

Lee, R. (2004). *The values of connection: A relational approach to ethics.* Hillsdale, NJ: Analytic Press.

Lewin, K. (1918). Kriegslandschaft [War landscape]. *Zeitschrift für Angewandte Psychologie, 12*, 440–453.

Lewin, K. (1936). *Principles of topological psychology*. New York, NY: McGraw-Hill. doi:10.1037/10019-000

Lewin, K. (1951). *Field theory in social science*. New York, NY: Harper & Brothers.

Lichtenberg, P. (1990). *Community and confluence: Undoing the clinch of oppression*. Cambridge, MA: GestaltPress.

Luborsky, L., Rosenthal, R., Diguer, L., Andrusyna, T. P., Berman, J. S., Levitt, J. T., . . . & Krause, E. D. (2002). The Dodo bird verdict is alive and well—mostly. *Clinical Psychology: Science and Practice, 9*, 2–12. doi.org/10.1093/clipsy/9.1.2

Marrow, A. (1969). *The practical theorist: The life and work of Kurt Lewin*. New York, NY: Basic Books.

McConville, M. (1995). *Adolescence: Psychotherapy and the emergent self*. San Francisco, CA: Jossey-Bass.

Melnick, J., & Nevis, S. M. (1994). Intimacy and power in long-term relationships: A gestalt therapy-systems perspective. In G. Wheeler & S. Backman (Eds.), *On intimate ground: A gestalt approach to working with couples*. San Francisco, CA: Jossey-Bass.

Miller, S., Wampold, B., & Varhely, K. (2008). Direct comparison of treatment modalities for youth disorders: A meta-analysis. *Psychotherapy Research, 18*, 5–14. doi.org/10.1080/10503300701472131

Nevis, E. C. (1987). *Organizational consulting: A gestalt approach*. Cleveland, OH: Gestalt Institute of Cleveland Press.

Norcross, J. C. (2011). *Psychotherapy relationships that work: Evidence-based responsiveness*. New York, NY: Oxford University Press. doi:10.1093/acprof:oso/9780199737208.001.0001

Oaklander, V. (2006). *Hidden treasure: A map to the child's inner self*. London, England: Karnac Books.

Panksepp, J. (2009). Brain, emotional systems and qualities of life: From animal model of affect to implications for psychotherapeutics. In D. Fosha, D. Siegel, & M. Solomon (Eds.), *The healing power of emotion: Affect neuroscience, development and practice*. New York, NY: Norton.

Parlett, M. (1992). Reflections on field theory. *British Gestalt Journal, 1*(2), 69–81.

Parlett, M. (in press). *Future present*. New York, NY: Routledge Taylor & Francis.

Pavlov, I. (1897). *The work of the digestive glands*. London, England: Griffin.

Perls, F. S. (1947). *Ego hunger and aggression: A critique of Freud's theory and method*. London, England: Allen & Unwin.

Perls, F. S. (1969). *In and out the garbage pail*. Moab, UT: Real People Press.

Perls, F. S., Hefferline, R., & Goodman, P. (1951). *Gestalt therapy: Excitement and growth in the human personality.* New York, NY: Julian Press.

Perls, L. (1992). *Living at the boundary.* Gouldsboro, ME: The Gestalt Journal Press.

Polster, E., & Polster, M. (1974). *Gestalt therapy integrated: Contours of theory and practice.* New York, NY: Vintage.

Polster, E., & Polster, M. (1999). *From the radical center: The heart of gestalt therapy.* Cleveland, OH: Gestalt Institute of Cleveland Press.

Reich, W. (1945). *Character analysis.* New York, NY: Farrar, Straus & Giroux.

Resneck-Sannes, H. (2011). Psychobiology of affects: Implications for a somatic psychotherapy. In V. Heinrich-Clauer (Ed.), *Handbook bioenergetic analysis* (pp. 429–440). Giessen, Germany: Psychosozial-Verlag.

Roberts, A. (1999). The field talks back: Field theory, constructivism and the retrieval of experience. *British Gestalt Journal, 8,* 35–46.

Russell, B. (2004). *History of western philosophy.* London, England: Routledge. (Original work published 1946)

Schore, A. N. (2003). *Affect regulation and the repair of the self.* New York, NY: Norton.

Schore, A. N. (2009). Relational trauma and the developing right brain: the neurobiology of broken attachment bonds. In T. Baradon (Ed.), *Relational trauma in infancy* (pp. 19–47). London, England: Routledge.

Schore, J. R., & Schore, A. N. (2008). Modern attachment theory: The central role of affect regulation in development and treatment. *Clinical Social Work Journal, 36,* 9–20. doi:10.1007/s10615-007-0111-7

Siegel, D. (2010). *The mindful therapist: A clinician's guide to mindsight and neural integration.* New York, NY: Norton.

Siegel, D. (2012). *The developing mind: How relationships and the brain interact to shape who we are.* New York, NY: Guildford Press.

Smith, M. L., & Glass, G. V. (1977). Meta-analysis of psychotherapy outcome studies. *American Psychologist, 32,* 752–760. doi:10.1037/0003-066X.32.9.752

Spagnuolo Lobb, M. (2013). *The now-for-next in psychotherapy: Gestalt therapy recounted in post-modern society.* Milan, Italy: FrancoAngeli.

Stevens, C., Stringfellow, J., Wakelin, K., & Waring, J. (2011). The UK gestalt psychotherapy CORE Research Project: The findings. *British Gestalt Journal, 20,* 22–27.

Stiles, W. B., Barkham, M., Mellor-Clark, J., & Connell, J. (2008). Effectiveness of cognitive-based, person-centered, and psychodynamic therapies in UK primary-care routine practice: Replication in a larger sample. *Psychological Medicine, 38,* 677–688. doi:10.1017/S0033291707001511

Stoehr, T. (Ed.). (1994a). *Crazy hope and finite experience: Final essays of Paul Goodman.* San Francisco, CA: Jossey-Bass/GestaltPress.

Stoehr, T. (1994b). *Here now next: Paul Goodman and the origins of gestalt therapy.* San Francisco, CA: Jossey-Bass/GestaltPress.

Stolorow, R. D., Atwood, G., & Orange, D. (2002). *World of experience: Interweaving philosophical and clinical dimensions in psychoanalysis.* New York, NY: Basic Books.

Strümpfel, U. (2006). *Therapie der Gefühle—Forschungsbefunde zur Gestalttherapie* [Therapy of emotions—Research findings on gestalt therapy]. Bergisch Gladbach, Germany: Verlag Andreas Kohlhage.

Tronick, E. (2007). *The neurobehavioral and social-emotional development of infants and children.* New York, NY: Norton.

Ullman, D. (2005, October). *Kurt Lewin: Bridging the gorge between psychology and social activism.* Paper presented at The Roots of Gestalt II, Antwerp, Belgium.

van der Kolk, B. (2005). Developmental trauma disorder: Toward a rational diagnosis for children with complex trauma histories. *Psychiatric Annals, 35,* 401–408.

van der Kolk, B. (2006). *Traumatic stress: The effects of overwhelming experience on mind, body and society.* New York, NY: Guildford Press.

Wampold, B. (2001). *The great psychotherapy debate: Models, methods and findings.* Mahwah, NJ: Erlbaum.

Wertheimer, M. (1912). Experimente studien ueber das sehen von bewegungen [Experimental studies in the perception of motion]. *Zeitschrift fur Psychologie mit Zeitschrift fur Angewandte Psychologie, 61,* 11–38.

Wertheimer, M. (1925, December). *Über Gestalttheorie* [About gestalt theory]. Paper presented at the meeting of the Kant Society, Berlin, Germany.

Wertheimer, M. (1938). Gestalt theory. In W. Ellis (Ed.), *A source book in gestalt psychology* (pp. 1–11). London, England: Routledge Kegan Paul. doi:10.1037/11496-001

Wertheimer, M. (1945). *Productive thinking.* Chicago, IL: University of Chicago Press.

Wheeler, G. (1989). *Love, work, and play: Essays in gestalt work with children.* Cambridge, MA: GestaltPress.

Wheeler, G. (1991). *Gestalt reconsidered: A new approach to contact and resistance.* New York, NY: Gardner Press/GestaltPress.

Wheeler, G. (1996). Self and shame: A new paradigm for psychotherapy. In R. Lee & G. Wheeler (Eds.), *The voice of shame: Silence and connection in psychotherapy* (pp. 23–60). San Francisco, CA: Jossey-Bass.

Wheeler, G. (1997). Self and shame: A Gestalt approach. *Gestalt Review, 1,* 221–244.

Wheeler, G. (2000). *Beyond individualism: Toward a new understanding of self, relation, and experience.* Hillsdale, NJ: Analytic Press.

Wheeler, G. (2003). Contact and creativity: The gestalt cycle in context. In M. Spagnuolo Lobb & N. Amendt-Lyon (Eds.), *Creative license: The art of gestalt therapy* (pp. 163–178). Wien, Austria: Springer-Verlag. doi:10.1007/ 978-3-7091-6023-7_14

Wheeler, G. (2004). Spirit and shadow: Esalen and gestalt. In G. W. Shuck & J. J. Kripal (Eds.), *On the edge of the future: Esalen Institute and the human potential movement.* Bloomington: Indiana University Press.

Wheeler, G. (2008). The age of complexity: Paul Goodman in the 21st century— A critical assessment. *Gestalt Review, 10,* 206–227.

Wheeler, G. (2011). Who are we? Narrative, evolution and development: Our stories and ourselves. In R. Lee & N. Harris (Eds.), *Relational child, relational brain: Development and therapy in childhood and adolescence* (pp. 5–54). New York, NY: Routledge Taylor & Francis.

Wilson, C. M., & Oswald, A. J. (2005). *How does marriage affect physical and psychological health? A survey of the longitudinal evidence.* Bonn, Germany: Institute for the Study of Labor.

Wilson, D. S. (2007). *Evolution for everyone: How Darwin's theory can change the way we think about our lives.* New York, NY: Delacorte Press.

Wundt, W. (2009). *Principles of physiological psychology.* New York, NY: General Books. (Original work published 1904)

Wysong, J., & Rosenfeld, E. (1982). *An oral history of gestalt therapy.* Highland, NY: Center for Gestalt Development.

Yontef, G. M. (1993). *Awareness, dialogue and process.* Highland, NY: Gestalt Journal Press.

Young, J. (1999). *Cognitive therapy for personality disorders: A schema-focused approach.* Sarasota, FL: Professional Resource Press.

Zaretskii, V. (2009). The zone of proximal development: What Vygotsky did not have time to write. *Journal of Russian and East European Psychology, 47*(6), 70–93. doi:10.2753/RPO1061-0405470604

Zinker, J. (1978). *Creative process in gestalt therapy.* New York, NY: Random House.

Index

Gaudiano, B. A., 112
Genuineness, 115
Gestalt Institute of Cleveland (GIC), 52–57
"Gestaltists," 9
Gestalt laws of perception, 18–19
Gestalt psychology, 9–28
  and associationism, 10–14
  development of therapy based on, 26–27. *See also* Gestalt therapy
  early applications of, 22–26
  early practitioners of, 14–21
  and scientific psychology, 10
Gestalts
  defined, 18
  fixed, 128
  subjective construction of, 23
  of understanding, 32
Gestalt theory. *See* Theory behind Gestalt therapy
Gestalt therapy, 29–69
  active nature of, 29, 39–43
  early history of, 27–28
  forms of awareness in, 38–39, 72–73
  impact of, 68–69
  psychological theory behind, 3–4
  research on outcomes of, 113–117
Gestalt Therapy: Novelty, Excitement, and Growth (Paul Goodman, Ralph Hefferline & Fritz Perls), 28, 50, 51
GIC (Gestalt Institute of Cleveland), 52–57
Goal collaboration, 115
Goodman, Paul
  on analytic interpretations, 34
  and balance between conservation and spontaneity, 30
  and client's contact patterns, 35, 36
  and creation of Gestalt therapy, 27–28
  definition of ego function provided by, 51
  and embodiment, 37
  and experiments in therapy, 40
  on Freudian patients, 45
  on full contact, 56
  on function of therapy, 31
  on gestalts of understanding, 32
  and ideal of health, 43
  importance of personal history to, 44
  and patient resistance, 46–49
  retirement of, from clinical work, 50
  and "safe emergency" concept, 36–37, 91
Group dynamics, 22
Group Dynamics Lab (Massachusetts Institute of Technology), 26

Health
  in Gestalt theory, 43–44
  in relational field model, 60–61
"Here-and-now," 68–69
History. *See* Gestalt psychology
History of Gestalt therapy, 9–28
  associationism, 10–14
  development of, 26–27
  early applications, 22–26
  early practitioners, 14–21
  scientific psychology, 10
Hycner, R., 58

Idealism, 9–10
Individualistic culture, 67, 129
Informal experiments, 40
Interaction, principles of, 13
Interactionist field models, 56
Interdependence, 49
Interpersonal psychotherapy, 114
Interpretation, with perception, 19–20
Intersubjectivity, 58
Intimacy, 90–92, 95

About the Authors

Gordon Wheeler, PhD, is a licensed psychologist with many years' experience writing, teaching, training, and practicing using a contemporary field-relational Gestalt therapy model. He is the author or editor of numerous books and articles in the field, most recently, *CoCreating the Field: Intention and Practice in the Age of Complexity* (with Deborah Ullman, 2009). Dr. Wheeler is on the visiting faculty of many Gestalt training institutes around the world, and is long-time president of the Esalen Institute in Big Sur, California, where he also served for some years as CEO. Together with Nancy Lunney Wheeler, he teaches Gestalt Relational Constellations widely around the world. His private practice of coaching, counseling, psychotherapy, and consulting is located in Santa Cruz, California. He can be contacted at gordon.wheeler@esalen.org.

Lena Axelsson, PsyD, was educated and received her Gestalt training in Sweden, moving to the United States in 2000. Following 4 years living and studying at Esalen Institute in Big Sur, California, she completed her doctoral work at Ryokan College, where her dissertation was *The Use of Relational Gestalt Therapy Informed by Neuroscience in the Treatment of Single Event and Developmental Trauma*. After serving for several years as a clinician and a clinical supervisor at Pajaro Valley Prevention and Student Assistance Center, working with troubled young people and families in a diverse population, Dr. Axelsson entered private clinical practice with children, adolescents, adults, couples and families. In addition to her clinical Gestalt training, she has also trained extensively with Peter Levine in Somatic Experiencing. She presents regularly at conferences and in training sessions on Gestalt-based multicultural work, as well as on single event and developmental trauma and the neuroscientific basis of contemporary Gestalt-based trauma and recovery work. Dr. Axelsson presents as well as part of the faculty of the Esalen Institute Evolution of Gestalt Symposium Series (selected proceedings published in the GestaltPress book series). Her forthcoming work on this topic as applied to couples work will appear in *The Couple in the Relational Field* (Eds. M. Kraus, A. Roberts, & G. Wheeler, in press). Dr. Axelsson lives in Santa Cruz, California, where she practices as a member of an integrative medical health team. Her special interests include hiking, running, and the diverse cuisines of Europe and the Americas. She can be contacted at lena.axelsson@comcast.net.

About the Series Editors

Jon Carlson, PsyD, EdD, ABPP, is distinguished professor, psychology and counseling at Governors State University and a psychologist at the Wellness Clinic in Lake Geneva, Wisconsin. Dr. Carlson has served as editor of several periodicals including the *Journal of Individual Psychology* and *The Family Journal.* He holds Diplomates in both family psychology and Adlerian psychology. He has authored or coauthored 175 journal articles and 60 books, including *Time for a Better Marriage, Adlerian Therapy, Inclusive Cultural Empathy, The Mummy at the Dining Room Table, Bad Therapy, The Client Who Changed Me, Their Finest Hour, Creative Breakthroughs in Therapy, Moved by the Spirit, Duped: Lies and Deception in Psychotherapy, Never Be Lonely Again, Helping Beyond the Fifty Minute Hour, Psychopathology and Psychotherapy, How Master Therapists Work: Effecting Change From the First Through the Last Session and Beyond,* and *On Being a Master Therapist: Practicing What You Preach.* He has created over 300 professional trade video and DVDs with leading professional therapists and educators. In 2004 the American Counseling Association named him a "Living Legend." In 2009 the Division of Psychotherapy of the American Psychological Association (APA) named him "Distinguished Psychologist" for his life contribution to psychotherapy, and in 2011 he received the APA Distinguished Career Contribution to Education and Training Award. He has received similar awards from four other professional organizations.

Matt Englar-Carlson, PhD, is a professor of counseling at California State University–Fullerton. He is a fellow of Division 51 of the American Psychological Association (APA). As a scholar, teacher, and clinician, Dr. Englar-Carlson has been an innovator and professionally passionate about training and teaching clinicians to work more effectively with their male clients. He has more than 30 publications and 50 national and international presentations, most of which are focused on men and masculinity and diversity issues in psychological training and practice. Dr. Englar-Carlson coedited the books *In the Room With Men: A Casebook of Therapeutic Change* and *Counseling Troubled Boys: A Guidebook for Professionals* and was featured in the 2010 APA-produced DVD *Engaging Men in Psychotherapy.* In 2007, he was named Researcher of the Year by the Society for the Psychological Study of Men and Masculinity. He is also a member of the APA Working Group to Develop Guidelines for Psychological Practice With Boys and Men. As a clinician, he has worked with children, adults, and families in school, community, and university mental health settings.